THE A
COOKBOOK

CREATIVE ACTIONS FOR A FAIR ECONOMY

UNITED FOR A FAIR ECONOMY

A HANDS-ON MANUAL FOR ORGANIZERS, ARTISTS AND EDUCATORS WHO WANT TO GET THEIR MESSAGE ACROSS IN POWERFUL, CREATIVE WAYS.

FOREWORD BY JIM HIGHTOWER

WRITTEN BY ANDREW BOYD

Table of Contents

Table of Contents

This book started out as a folder full of ideas and has grown. Andrew Boyd, the "minister of culture" for United for a Fair Economy, has carried the project—bringing his humor, grace and hard work to a cookbook we hope will infuse our social movements with spark and mischief.

This manual was a collective effort. All along the way there have been numerous readers, creative activists and friends who helped make it happen. Hearty thanks goes to:

The members of the Class Acts theater troupe who pre-tested and cooked many of these recipes.

Carin Schiewe and Lee Winkelman for being there for the author with emotional support and strategic advice during the dark moments when the muses turned away.

Rocky Delaplaine at the Labor Heritage Foundation for being a gateway to creativity in the labor movement.

Immeasurable thanks goes to all those who punched around the manuscript, including: Chuck Collins, Felice Yeskel, Lynn Carlile, Roger Kerson, Heather Gonzalez, Julie McCall, David Behrstock, Tara Mooney, Kosta Demos, Elaine Bernard, Joan Holden, Mike Prokosch, and Chris Hartman.

A special debt goes to those who gave freely of their ideas, stories, scripts and photo permissions: the United Steel Workers of America, M. A. Swedlund and the Fat Cats, Steve Collins and the Mass Human Services Coalition, Margaret Butler, Rodney Ward, INFACT, Guerrilla Girls & Voyager Co., Vale at RE/SEARCH, Dan Kaufman, Liz Canner, Attieno Davis, Simon Greer, Simone Albeck and Mary Eady.

And this manual wouldn't look like much more than a shabby rag with gray text if not for the incredible illustrations of Shannon Palmer, John Lapham, and Laura Beldavs and special photo contributions by Laura Wulf, Ellen Shub, Mike Massey, Tricia Brennan, John May, and the folks at Impact Visuals.

Also thanks goes to Tara Mooney for her willingness to offer up her original creative action ideas and theater games for public use and abuse and to David Behrstock for his relentless wrestling with art and propaganda.

And those who did the odd jobs: Michael Barrish, Harry Levinson, Seth Levy, Susan Gerner, Cynthia Ward, and Ken Porter.

Also we would like to give special recognition to the manuals and guidebooks upon whose shoulders this one was built: Street Theater and Other Outdoor Performance by Bim Mason, Culture Jamming by Mark Dery, the War Resisters League Organizer's Manual, Let the World Know by Jason Salzman, Organizing for Social Change put out by the Midwest Academy, Pranks! by RE/Search, the Billboard Liberation Front Manual, and the Guerrilla Media Guide to Newspaper Wraps.

This manual was made possible with funding support from the A. J. Muste Foundation, Haymarket People's Fund, the Ben and Jerry's Foundation, the Unitarian Universalist Funding Program and a number of wonderful individuals (you know who you are!).

To the streets!

—United for a Fair Economy

FOREWORD
JIM HIGHTOWER

Read
Enjoy
Agitate

December, 1996
Austin, TX

My momma always told me that two wrongs don't make a right—but I soon figured out that three left turns do.

A little spirited cleverness is what has often been the difference in our history between earnest, wrinkle-browed reform efforts that just sat there stewing in their own juices and those reform efforts that caught the imagination of a larger public and became movements that actually reformed something.

Yes, marching off to fight for economic fairness, social justice and equal opportunity for all is serious business, but "serious" doesn't demand "boring." That's why I like this cookbook of creative actions. It is filled with great ideas for making the progressive message...well, cook. I've been to many rallies and way too many conferences in my day convened by well-meaning, terribly serious folks truly trying to make a difference. But bless their hearts, someone had removed their funny bones and stolen their creative caps.

If we want to touch the hearts and minds of America (and we do) we need to unleash our imaginations, take creative risks, and explore new forms of communicating besides the lecture and press release. Our events should feed the soul as well as the brain, and we should laugh and celebrate even as we speak the truth. As an old Yugoslavian proverb puts it: "You can fight the gods and still have fun."

So, if you're turned off politics-as-usual, this cookbook might help you find a way to turn back on. If you don't believe a word anybody says on TV, this cookbook will get you making your own media. If you don't think you have a creative bone in your body, think again, this cookbook is for everyone.

Read. Enjoy. Agitate.

You must do that which you think you cannot do.

—ELEANOR ROOSEVELT

The artist is not a special kind of man, but every man is a special kind of artist.

—ANANDA COOMRASWAMY

Simon Greer, labor organizer.
"I work as a labor organizer in South Carolina. And I use theater a lot. But I don't think of myself as an "actor" or an "artist" except in the way that all of us are. I just strongly believe in the human ability to invent and imagine.

"I first got turned on to this stuff at a workshop seven years ago. We did an exercise in which each of us played out the same scene a number of times using seven different feelings or personalities. And then we played around with it. And I still think of acting as simply inviting one feeling or person to come out.

"But before this I was always terrified. *I can't act in front of people.* All the usual stuff. But this broke it all down. It turns out that it's easier to be on stage acting because you're not playing yourself. Your intelligence is not on the line. No one is asking, "Is he smart?", or whatever—because you're playing someone else. And you get to play people who you can't stand, and you get to ham it up. And it's easy because everyone knows the boss, and they love making fun of the boss. Or you're playing a scene of an organizer dealing with Black and White tensions and everyone recognizes it and thinks, *Oh God, here we are, again.* It becomes *their* experience. It's not, *Oh that panel was dull.* Instead, people are much more forgiving with this kind of theater. I still get nervous giving speeches, but not acting.

"It was exciting to watch myself go from being scared and nervous to 'OK, this is good.' "

"Also, I use theater as an organizing tool. Actors rehearse, right? Well, organizers need to rehearse too, maybe more so. It has actually made our work, not only more creative, but much more disciplined and effective. What is an action but a staged event with a lot of improvisation? Just like a lot of theater. Theater is a way of thinking. We didn't used to scope out sites but now we do. Now we ask, "When is the audience going to be there?"

Attieno Davis, community organizer.
"When the opportunity came along to do theater in the community, I had big fears. They

"I don't think of myself as an 'actor' or an 'artist' except in the way that all of us are."

Attieno performing the "Dance of the10 Chairs." *photo Mike Massey, 1996*

had to do with my own capacity. Could I act? Could I be part of something that was helping to shape community thought? And at the same time I saw that it would be fun. Over time, I found that I *could* do it. There was a strong sense that all of us were capable of contributing, that all of us could do any of it.

"It was exciting to watch myself go from being scared and nervous to "OK, this is good." It just felt good. I can't use any other words, because it would get too personal. It felt good. All of it felt good.

Mary Eady, labor educator, retired.

" I was self-conscious, but I joined in with the rest of the group... and I've never been quite the same."

"I used to be quite shy. But at a key moment in my life someone made me get up out of my chair and play around. It was in a social drama class. I was self-conscious but I joined in with the rest of the group in a bunch of games and skits and I've never been quite the same. There's something about it. Getting people moving, role-playing, using their bodies and voices—you release something in the group that you don't by just talking.

"I've been doing adult education work with unions ever since. I'm retired now but I still do this work because it feeds me. People retire but the issues don't. I'm still active.

We have no art. We do everything as well as we can.

—BALINESE SAYING

Simone Albeck, student and activist. "Working on a creative political project with other people is very affirming. When there's ten people all around you, also making fools of themselves, there's no more being on the fence. You jump in, and it's OK. The creativity was in me all along, but supported by the group, I felt the confidence and enough safety to bring it out.

Simone in her kitchen. *photo Laura Wulf, 1997*

"And the people you're trying to reach are so receptive. You don't have to start from zero like you often do when you're leafleting. It's just a great way to do politics.

"And there's something really peaceful about it. It's not about competing. It's very healthy. It's about discovering what you have to say and saying it. It's exciting—you're creating something that didn't exist before. It gives you a feeling of possibility and thus of hope...

"The creativity was in me all along, and supported by the group, I felt the confidence and enough safety to bring it out."

In the spring of 1993, the Communication Workers of America were in the final stages of a five year effort to organize 1700 clerical and technical workers on the campus of Indiana University. Although nearly half the full-time staff qualified for food stamps and other forms of public assistance, a large share of workers were not responding. Organizers needed a creative way to juice up the energy of the election, appeal to disinterested workers, and turn out the vote in big numbers.

Their answer: Elvis Presley. Organizers hired a professional Elvis impersonator and rewrote a series of Elvis songs to carry the union message, including "Heartbreak Payroll" and the Vegas crooning song, "Now or Never," which became the theme of the campaign. The pro-union Elvis was featured on billboards and radio ads and went along on work site visits. Workers who wouldn't look up from their desks in the past would chase him down the hall to sign their union literature. The campus was a buzz with "Elvis sightings." On election eve, he was also the featured guest at a huge get out the vote rally. The union won by a landslide, 1005 to 250.

In the early 80's, to help sell the idea of "trickle-down" economics to the public, the American Conservative Union held a gala dinner featuring the world's largest pie. Over 17 feet across, the pie was to be sliced and distributed to all in attendance as a way of demonstrating that "everyone will get a piece of the pie."

Five members of the Community for Creative Non-Violence, wearing oversize business suits and name tags of Reagan's wealthy friends, walked into the party and jumped into the pie. With the TV cameras rolling, they slopped around in the pie goop, slinging it around at each other, screaming, "It's all for me! It's all for me!" To get them out, security guards had to wade into the pie themselves. The event was ruined, and that night an incredible image of greed run amok was beamed out to living rooms across America.

In the early 90's, labor activists in Baltimore were outraged at the huge government subsidies that downtown corporations had received. Activists organized a "sightseeing tour" of the worst offenders and invited the community and media along. At each stop, with the target site in the background, folks held up huge dollar signs and numbers on placards, making it very clear who was getting welfare and exactly how much. The media loved it.

In 1994, TV stations all across the country were refusing to air Deadly Deception, the Academy Award winning film exposing GE's involvement in the nuclear weapons industry. To protest this censorship, activists from Paper Tiger and FAIR projected the

entire film onto the side of the Bay Area KQED TV building and invited the community into the streets for the evening's entertainment. The station relented and aired the film.

A strange figure stood outside the supermarket, dressed in a jester's hat and costume with a painted face and a big cardboard house worn about his torso. Silent as a mime, he gave out leaflets and little plastic houses with a tiny message wrapped up inside each, such as: "Know your rights #3. If there are bad conditions in your apartment you may be able to stop a rent increase. Collect all 17!" On the back, the messages were also in Spanish.

Why should we all use our creative power...? Because there is nothing that makes people so generous, joyful, lively, bold, and compassionate, so indifferent to...the accumulation of objects and money.

BRENDA UELAND

Children gathered around, tugging on their parents sleeves to look at him and read his messages. Who was this masked man? He was the "Housing Jester," a brainchild of the Boston housing group, City Life, and the mascot of their upcoming Affordable Housing Festival. The word got out, local media picked up the image, attendance at the event was high.

Woody Allen says that "90% of life is just showing up." What he forgets is that the other 10% makes all the difference. Okay, so you've shown up. Now what do you do? That's the question this cookbook tries to answer. If the pie-wreckers had crashed the party with the standard placards and slogans, they would have been discreetly escorted out the door. If the housing jester hadn't changed costume on his way to the supermarket, sure, people would have taken the leaflets but they wouldn't have been charmed or intrigued. If the film activists had held a private protest screening or if the tour organizers had held a standard rally, there would have been no direct dramatic challenge to the target, no media spectacle, and consequently, a lot less pressure.

This cookbook is full of action ideas like the ones above that will help you creatively fight back against corporate greed.

For the last twenty years, there has been an all out "class war" against the economic security of working people in this country. Workers are losing ground and poor people are being scapegoated for these bad economic policies.

A movement is building for greater economic fairness. Workers are building alliances with communities and forming worker centers to stand up for their rights. The organized labor movement is newly energized and putting more resources into organizing and economics education. Grassroots political groups are focusing on economic justice. Immigrant groups and welfare recipients are standing up to say they will not be scapegoated.

At the heart of any movement, any *moving* of people, is art and culture. Imagine the civil rights movement without song. Imagine the labor movement without murals and creative street actions. Imagine the peace movement without giant Bread and Puppet figures floating above a rally. Imagine the populist farm movements without weekend encampments, song and theater. Imagine the movement for gay and lesbian rights without creative posters, graphics and "A Day Without Art" events.

This cookbook is for people engaged in these struggles. It is overflowing with ideas for creative action—ideas that can stir up the brainstorms already percolating in your own imaginations. Like a real cookbook, sometimes just seeing a recipe makes your mouth water. The mere suggestion gets you thinking about something you want to cook and eat, even if you don't follow the recipe.

And for those of you who are saying, *...this isn't for me, I'm not an artist, I get stage fright, I can't draw, I can't sing, I'm not creative, I have no talent...*, think about this: if you have ever been to a demonstration or carried a placard or raised your arms or voice in protest, you've already done political theater, you've already done a creative action in public. Talent is not some elusive quality that some have and others don't. Everybody has something to offer. Being creative means being resourceful, open to alternatives and possibilities. It means being committed to your inner vision. Art isn't something rich people do with their leisure time—it's something working people do with their lives.

This manual is designed to help you put on creative actions around issues of growing inequality in the US. It is written in a modular fashion: you can read it straight through or dip in anywhere. We suggest you approach it in the same spirit you might approach a cookbook: as an inventory of possibilities, an introduction to unfamiliar cuisines, a handbook of the tools of the trade.

This cookbook is brought to you by Art for a Fair Economy, a growing network of artists and activists from diverse class backgrounds seeking creative ways to reach people and challenge the cultural myths that support economic inequality.

We are part of United for a Fair Economy (formerly Share the Wealth), a national organization that draws public attention to the growth of income and wealth inequality in the US—and to the implications of this inequality for American life and labor. We provide popular education resources, work with grassroots organizations, conduct research, support legislative action to reduce inequality and undertake creative direct actions.

There's a lot in this cookbook—something for everyone. Use it; play with it; cook up trouble with it; pass it around—and please, make a little history with it wherever you can.

To whet your appetite, we offer you our tiny manifesto:

ART IS FOR THE REST OF US

ART IS NOT A COMMODITY OR A PLAYTHING OF CORPORATE POWER • ART IS FOR THE REST OF US • art for the rest of us TRANSFORMS THE WORLD • art for the rest of us CAN BE MADE BY "NON-ARTISTS" • art for the rest of us IS POLITICAL WITHOUT BEING HEAVY-HANDED • art for the rest of us CAN LIVEN UP DRY ECONOMIC DATA AND TELL A STORY • art for the rest of us CAN REACH PEOPLE WHO WOULD OTHERWISE BE TURNED OFF • art for the rest of us IS EMPOWERING • art for the rest of us BUILDS COMMUNITY • art for the rest of us IS FUN, PROVOCATIVE, AND ACCESSIBLE • art for the rest of us IS BY, FOR AND OF THE REST OF US

No revolutionary movement is complete without its poetic expression. If such a movement has caught hold of the imagination of the masses they will seek a vent in song for the aspirations, fears, and hopes, the loves and hatreds engendered by the struggle. Until the movement is marked by the joyous, defiant singing of revolutionary songs, it lacks one of the most distinctive marks of a popular revolutionary movement: it is the dogma of the few and not the faith of the multitude.

—JAMES CONNOLLY, 1907
IRISH REVOLUTIONARY

Art is not a mirror to reflect reality but a hammer with which to change it.

—BERTOLT BRECHT

Creative actions come in all shapes, sizes and flavors, from street theater skits to guerrilla leafleting, to media hoaxes. Here we present a sampling of some of the major cuisines, arranged in order from most familiar to most exotic.

Think of this list as a menu of possibilities. Use it to stretch your imagination.

Popular Theater

People all over the world are taking back theater to explore issues that are relevant to them and their communities. Popular theater encompasses a range of forms and movements. In general, it is non-commercial, rooted in community and struggle, and often done on the cheap, using local materials. It often challenges the boundaries between actor and non-actor, and performer and audience. the Bread and Puppet Theater, the San Francisco Mime Troupe, In the Heart of the Beast, The Los Angeles Poverty Department, and the work of Augusto Boal and his Theater of the Oppressed are all part of this broader movement.

Street Theater

Throughout history and in many cultures, the medium of "the street," or common public space, has served as a venue for creatively voicing concerns. It is both immediate and affordable. Some common forms of street theater include:

Sidewalk skits. Short skits performed on a sidewalk, street-corner or public square.

Processions. Pageants, parades and costumed processions down the street, often with music and big puppets, sometimes festive, sometimes somber.

Spectacles. Large-scale performances such as the outdoor version of the 100 Chairs (see Chapter 8: Complete Recipes).

Ritual performances. Deeply symbolic performances with ritual-like rhythms and atmosphere. Can also be punchy adaptations of standard ritual formats, such as alternative shrines or mock exorcisms, funerals, incantations, etc.

Guerrilla Leafleting
Using theater to leaflet is a fun and effective way to distribute information. In the 80's, activists opposed to US military intervention in Central America dressed up as waiters and carried maps of the war in Central America on serving trays. They went up to people in the street and said, "Excuse me, did you order this war?" and then followed up with an itemized bill and the line, "Well, you paid for it."

Saturation Postering ("Sniping")
Pasting up posters or stenciling graffiti late at night in public spaces is known as sniping. Saturation Postering takes sniping to a whole new level. A good example of this is Poster Nation, a coordinated nationwide postering campaign begun by students at Wesleyan University and now organized by United for a Fair Economy.

On a few key days each year (Tax Day, Labor Day, Election Day, etc.), activists post a similar set of posters in public places all over the country. The campaign is coordinated in an open-ended, decentralized fashion over the Internet. The Poster Nation web page (www.stw.org/posters) allows you to join the campaign, view and download any of the current posters, offer new posters of your own invention, as well as locate other people in your area who are active in the campaign.

This kind of structure can achieve a strong, nationally coordinated message focus and at the same time, provide a great degree of freedom and creativity to local artists and activists. With the web address and a tiny explanation on every poster, the campaign can grow like a virus. (For more information on Poster Nation, see Chapter 10: Keeping the Kitchen Stocked.)

If you don't like the news, go out and make some of your own.

—Wes "Scoop" Nisker

Death gives Phillip Morris some bad press, New York City, 1996. *photo Karla Capers, INFACT.*

Media Stunts
A media stunt is a creative event with a strong symbolic hook designed to focus the attention of the media on your issue. Understanding what the media wants is important in getting coverage. Editors are looking for a short punchy event in which everyday people, who are like their own audience, do something visually interesting. This doesn't have to be a funny gimmick—it can also be a dramatic way of showing the seriousness of the problem. Here are a some of

To move the media, you must communicate as responsible extremists, not as reasonable moderates.

—Public Media Center

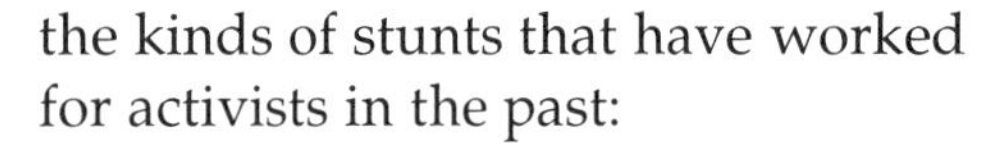

the kinds of stunts that have worked for activists in the past:

Dramatize a phrase. One candidate held a press conference outside a waffle house to dramatize how his opponent was "waffling" on the issues; clean government activists in Maine held an event with over 25 kites in the air, telling big money lobbyists to "go fly a kite."

Hand out symbols not just leaflets. Handing out flyers rarely attracts the media. AIDS activists have handed out condoms and environmental activists, gas masks.

Do a real stunt. Sometimes, just doing a real stunt at the right time and place can draw a story: one activist got his picture and his issue in the paper by climbing a tree and talking to reporters on his cell phone, others have parachuted into outdoor events, dangled from buildings, immersed themselves in tubs of jello, etc.

"Ban the Burn." Greenpeace hangs a banner on a Michigan smoke stack to protest acid rain in the Great Lakes region, 1994. *photo Marc PoKempener, Impact Visuals*

Send a unique message. Instead of sending just letters to a target, send a symbolic item such as a container of contaminated water or a chunk of government cheese.

Hold a contest or an art show. Put out a call to local artists for "Art for a Fair Economy" and hold a show. Or ask kids to draw images of fair and unfair worlds or economies.

Drop a banner. An ordinary banner in an extraordinary place can draw the media. Greenpeace has hung a "Next Time Try Recycling" banner on a toxic barge in New York harbor, and a "World Bankenstein" banner on the World Bank building in DC. Try hanging a "Cut Corporate Welfare" banner off a corporate skyscraper after a major round of downsizing. Highway overpasses are also good sites and much easier.

Create a symbol or replica of the problem. The 100 Chairs (see Chapter 8: Complete Recipes) is only one of many great examples. In the 80's students erected South African shantytowns on campuses all across the US. Environmental activists dumped a 20 foot high inflatable toxic waste barrel outside the Utah State Capitol to protest a proposed toxic waste dump. With each person adding one pair, the citizens of Paris assembled a tragically huge pile of shoes to commemorate all the victims of land mines. Ceramic artist Barbara Dornachy made a sculpture of 34,000 miniature bombers and missiles to dramatize the size of the US nuclear arsenal.

Guerrilla Theater

Peace and AIDS activists have staged mass "die-in's" which blocked street traffic or forced officials to pick their way through piles of "bodies" to get into their offices. Guerrilla theater intrudes into everyday public spaces, creatively interfering with business as usual. Guerrilla theater often uses a "stage" that is already charged with meaning and attention. Members of Border Arts in San Diego draw attention to immigration issues by trespassing onto Federal property to perform in the No Man's Land on the US-Mexico border.

In guerrilla theater, as in guerrilla warfare, combatants use small, quick, mobile actions to engage the public.

Or they appear by surprise, seize a strategic stage and hold it just long enough to accomplish their mission.

Guerrilla Projection

With a high-powered slide or movie projector, you can turn the side of a building into a huge advertisement for your cause. On the eve of the Great American Smokeout in 1994, INFACT hit the Philip Morris building in New York with images two stories tall and a running count of the number of kids addicted to cigarettes. The kind of slide projector you need is called a Xenon 750 and can be rented for $150 and up.

Newspaper Wraps & Inserts

Imagine opening up a street corner newspaper box, pulling out the local daily, sleepily looking it over and suddenly realizing that someone has switched the front page! Wraps and inserts are direct interventions into other publications. A wrap is a front (and back) page of your own invention that wraps around the target publication. An insert, maybe disguised as an extra section, slips inside.

By closely mimicking typeface and layout, wraps and inserts should seem, at least at first glance, like the real thing. After that there are two strategies: 1) blaring headlines with strongly worded information that a reader will very quickly realize is alien to the target publication or 2) a more subtle approach in which the reader only slowly begins to suspect that something is amiss. Often wraps and inserts are used to raise concerns about how the target publication is covering the issues.

Remember: the target publication will interpret any wrap or insert as a hostile action, trespassing, a violation of free speech, etc. So don't get caught or reveal your identity.

"Sun Mad." Anti-advertisement attacking agricultural pesticide practices.
1981 serigraph
Ester Hernandez

Anti-Advertisement

Imagine walking past a wall of poster ads in the subway and coming across one with a riderless horse grazing in a cemetery accompanied by the slogan, "Welcome to Marlboro Country." An anti-advertisement is an alternative advertisement that mocks and parodies a real ad. It can take any form a real ad takes: TV spot, magazine ad, poster, direct mail piece, etc. The idea is to very closely mimic the texture and components of the real ad but in some way twist the message around into a new and opposing meaning. The final product is either placed and paid for exactly as if it were a real ad or it can be circulated more informally, say as a postcard.

Free speech is the right to shout "theater" in a crowded fire.

—Yippie Proverb

...social movements...bring people together to name their experience and share stories. A sound bite is merely an extremely abbreviated from of story-telling.

—Charlotte Ryan

Billboard Correction
Imagine driving down the highway and seeing a huge billboard for Kool cigarettes but the "K" has been craftily

"A can of spray paint, a blithe spirit, and a balmy night ..." *photo Jill Posener*

changed to an "F," to spell "Fool." These "roadside advertising enhancements" have the advantage of simple tools (spray paint and a ladder), high-visibility, and a big public prank for all to see. According to the Billboard Liberation Front, "the most effective alterations are often the simplest. If you can totally change the meaning of an advert by changing one or two letters, you'll save a lot of time and trouble." Billboards are considered private property and altering them illegal. Proper attention should be given to security and avoiding arrest.

Theater is a vocation for all human beings: it is the true nature of humanity.

—AUGUSTO BOAL

Currency Hacking
Currency hacking is a way to circulate a message by putting it on cash. Generally this is done by stamping phrases in ink right across the face of the bills. For example, members of the gay rights movement have stamped "gay money" and "lesbian money" in bright pinks on bills to gain visibility and demonstrate the consumer clout of the gay community. For obvious reasons, currency hacking might be a particularly suitable way to carry a message about economic injustice. The stamp design could play off of icons and text already on the bill. Again, remember, any alteration of US currency is a Federal offense and we unswervingly plead with you not to do anything that even remotely resembles it.

Theater of the Oppressed
Described by its founder, Augusto Boal, as a "rehearsal for revolution," Theater of the Oppressed is a set of interactive theater games and techniques that allow an audience to intervene in open-ended performances. One of the goals is to break down the barrier between actor and spectator and have all participants become "spect-actors." Typically, the work is done in community, school or workplace settings and can take a number of forms:

Forum Theater. Performers act out a scene of oppression but leave it unresolved. The audience is invited to suggest and enact solutions. In this way the community can confront their oppression and test out ways of overcoming it. Theater becomes a medium in which to explore solutions to social problems.

Image Theater. Participants make still images of their lives, feelings, experiences and oppressions; groups suggest titles or themes, and individuals "sculpt" images under these titles, using their own and others' bodies as "clay."

Invisible Theater. Invisible Theater occurs in an everyday public space but remains "invisible" to the public: only the performers know a performance is taking place.

For example, a performer enters a grocery story, picks up some basic food items (rice, bread, beans, milk) but when it comes time to pay, tells the cashier she has no money. She insists she needs the food to feed herself and her family. The cashier responds; the scene evolves. Another performer joins in, saying she should be allowed to have the food. The manager arrives. Another performer goes off on a rant, saying she should be thrown out of the store.

Other performers, farther from the center of action, turn to their neighbors and remark upon the goings-on. The scene continues to evolve; real issues are confronted, yet the performance remains invisible to the public. Good invisible theater requires a detailed script and enough rehearsals to cover the many possible directions a performance might take.

Newspaper Theater
Newspaper Theater is a set of simple techniques for turning average news items into theatrical performances with a political edge.

Crossed reading. Two news items are read, alternating back and forth, each giving critical friction to the other.

Rhythmic reading. News is read to the rhythm of rock, rap, country, or Gregorian chant in such a way that the rhythm contradicts the story, revealing the news item's true agenda.

Parallel action: Actors mime actions while the news is read, showing the context in which the news really occurred. One hears the news but sees something else that complements it visually.

Text out of context: The news is presented out of the context in which it was published. For example, an actor gives the speech about austerity measures previously delivered by the Minister of Economics while he devours an enormous sandwich.

Instead of waging an all-out assault on the Castle, the prankster slips through the gates wearing a fool's outfit...

—ART TINNITUS

Commotions
In the mid 1960's, Abbie Hoffman and a few friends dumped a flurry of $1 dollar bills on the New York Stock Exchange. The ensuing commotion, with stock brokers scrambling and fighting each other all over the floor, brought trading to a halt and became an icon of what was wrong with American culture and how easily it could be fingered.

A commotion is powerful and dangerous for the same reason: other people are doing the performing. When your target makes your point for you, it can be very convincing. However, your target may not play the way you hope, so you need to be both crafty and responsible.

Pride Stamps.
Money talks—but what should it say?
photo Dan Kaufman Graphics

Provocations
In the 1960's the Provos, a group of Amsterdam radicals, disrupted the local automobile culture by blocking traffic. They also began to fill Amsterdam with "White Bicycles"—old bicycles, fixed up, painted white, and left on the streets for everybody to use. Their idea was that nobody owned the bicycles; people just rode them wherever they needed and left them for the next person.

A provocation always has two parts: a negative, direct attack on the target and a positive, playful "White Action" that offers a glimpse of a working alternative. The two work hand in hand.

Happenings

In 1967 Abbie Hoffman and 25,000 other protesters, many dressed as witches and warlocks and chanting incantations, encircled the Pentagon and tried to levitate it. National Guard units were given explicit instructions to at no time permit the protesters to make a complete linking of hands around the building.

Pranks are symbolic warfare.

—Abbie Hoffman

An action-oriented Happening is an absurd event that disarms and ridicules the target—almost by association. In Poland members of the Orange Alternative would gather at the Warsaw Zoo, hold hands around the Orangutan cage and sing Stalinist hymns. What could the Polish police do? Arrest them? For what?

Media Hoax

A media hoax is an elaborate ruse designed to entrap the media into covering a fictional story carefully constructed for them. Here's how it works: you invent a fictional entity, such as the "1% Club," an exclusive club for the very wealthy that meets in different places every Friday night for a "feast of destruction" at which each member tries to outdo the other by burning a greater amount of their own money.

By producing "evidence" that such a club exists: staged photos, an invitation on letterhead, an answering message, etc., you get an out of town paper to cover it sight unseen.

Now, with this clip, you "really" exist and you can go on to generate more substantial media. Maybe the story snowballs. At some point before the ruse is uncovered by others, you hold a press conference, reveal the deception, and draw attention both to the issue itself (in this example, the reality of obscene wealth) as well as cultural biases revealed in the process of the media's gullibility.

If this sounds far fetched, take inspiration from Joey Skaggs, a New York conceptual con artist, who invented a fictional pet brothel (yes, a pet brothel), which culminated in a prime-time ABC news segment that received an Emmy nomination for best news program of the year.

This chapter presents tactics and techniques that will help you devise, produce and perform your own creative actions.

PLANNING THE MENU

When you're putting together your own actions it really pays off to take a couple steps back and think through your goals and options. Consider how your action fits into the larger strategy or campaign you are involved in. Try to get clear on what are you trying to communicate and to whom. Think about what has and hasn't worked in the past. We offer the following questions as a guide.

Questions to Consider when Planning a Creative Action

1. Is there a political target? If so, what do they want? What are your goals? What pressure can you bring to bear?
2. Who's your audience? Is it the general population or a particular constituency?
3. Where does your audience gather? Union conferences, churches, public squares, rush hour subway stations, parades, cultural events? Indoors or outdoors?
4. What does your audience care about? Health care, daycare, job cuts, welfare?
5. What message, style and mode of delivery will be most effective at reaching your audience (given who they are, where they are and what they care about)? Will it be direct (live) or indirect (via the media)? Subtle and sophisticated or more straightforward? Aggressive and challenging or more gentle? Straight or satirical?
6. Are you attempting to nourish and reinforce an audience that already substantially agrees with you or are

you trying to persuade and educate an audience with more neutral or mixed opinions? Do you and your audience talk about things in the same way?

7. Is the action fun? Does it demonstrate real power? Does it raise the morale of your own people? Is it likely to get media coverage?

Not only must great ideas have wings, they must also have landing gears.

—UNKNOWN

It is important to be very clear about who your audience is. Different kinds of actions have different kinds of audiences. If you are demonstrating outside a corporate HQ or disrupting the office of an elected official, then you've got to consider two audiences: the political target whose behavior you want to influence, and the regular audience (onlookers and observers via the media), whose understanding and support you want to gain. You need to think about how your action will affect both of these audiences.

In Rhode Island, a group of public housing tenants who were being stonewalled in their attempt to set up a community day care facility, walked into the housing authority and set up an ad-hoc day care facility right in the middle of the director's office—complete with children, caretakers, and toys. The organizers of this action understood that they had two audiences and devised an action that spoke powerfully to both by fusing symbolism with political pressure.

The truth is more important than the facts.

—FRANK LLOYD WRIGHT

Actions like the ones above, are called *direct* actions because they *directly* challenge a political target. On the other hand, a street theater skit in the park or an indoor performance at a union hall is not a direct action. There is no confrontation with a political target and the only audience is right there in front of you, watching. Here your primary purpose is to bring a message before the public, and to educate and inspire.

In spite of the differences between these two kinds of actions, you will find that many of the tactics and techniques described in the next sections apply to both, though maybe in different ways. Keep this in mind as you read through the next sections.

Designing the Action-Performance

There are no hard and fast rules on how to design an effective creative action. By nature, creativity is open-ended and experimental. An action is a unique encounter between your group's style and imagination and an issue and audience. However, in spite of this great variety, creative approaches draw upon a common pool of possibilities—humor, parody, surprise, hidden identity—which have political uses and limits. With this in mind, we offer some general guidelines which we find broadly useful.

Less Is More. Everyone forgets this one, newcomers and veterans alike. It's called "message discipline" and the key word here is discipline. You've got a lot to say, sure. The world needs to hear it, sure. But figure out what is the ONE thing you need to say, then say it well and repeat it over and over. You can say the next one thing next time.

Keep text to a minimum. Nothing is more deadly than lots of text without interruption. Whatever it is—performance, pamphlet, or vigil—make it visual or physical or musical. If there's data, illustrate it. Remember, in today's TV world, image is king. This is doubly good advice outdoors, where spoken words are often lost in other noise.

Maintain a consistent look and feel. All parts of the action should present a single theme in a consistent way. The design of any slogans, phrases, flyer graphics, banners, theatrical props, press releases should all be coordinated to develop a single message and visual identity.

Use powerful metaphors. Portray the economy as a game with unfair rules. Use a fashion show to expose sweatshops. Use metaphors and motifs that are common in the culture and rework them to carry your message.

Don't Laundry List. Be inclusive, yes, but don't feel like you have to mention every identity constituency in each and every performance. You are telling a story, not an agenda. People will find a way to connect. Likewise, when talking about the future, don't feel compelled to mention every item on the progressive wish list. You are sharing a vision, not a platform.

Offer vision not complaints. Convey hope and offer doable alternatives. Show people that it *can* be done and how. When appropriate, offer specific and tangible proposals for change. Think of yourself more as a messenger of hope than a conveyor of information.

Don't Preach. Everyone knows the unpleasantness of being preached at. Try to embed the important information right in the performance. Avoid lecturing. Avoid having characters that feel like they are being set up and fed speechifying words. Try to show more and tell less—the audience will teach themselves.

Make it Subtle or Make it Clear? You can use melodrama, oversized caricatures, and labels pinned onto costumes, to bluntly pit good against evil. Or you can take a more subtle approach, giving the audience more room to draw their own conclusions.

Balance Art and Message. When creating political art there is often a tension between the art part and the politics part. The art wants to explore the deep questions. The politics insists on a clear direction and message. Sometimes quick and dirty creative gimmicks are the order of the day. But sometimes it pays to try and go deeper.

Bread & Puppet Theater brings its special brand of symbolism to DC to protest the Gulf War, 1991
photo Ellen Shub

The highest challenge for the cultural activist is to create a powerful work of art that still conveys a clear political message. To do this you need to get past the surface conversation and into the deeper human concerns that lie at the heart of the issue. This means that the person creating the art has to find a way into that deeper place inside them that is connected to the issue—and then find a way to carry that back to the world.

If I could tell you what it meant, there would be no point in dancing it.

—Isadora Duncan

The unconscious wants truth. It ceases to speak to those who want something else more than truth.

—Adrienne Rich

Life comes before politics and politics is rooted in and arises out of life. In order to find and speak our truths, each of us needs to seek out the life sources of our politics. If we want to touch our audience, we must first get in touch with ourselves.

(The theater games showcased later in this chapter are one way to help this process along.)

Combine Serious and Satirical Approaches. Two anti-sweatshop organizers were invited onto a radio talk show. One played it straight, the other impersonated a character: U. R. Conned, President & CEO of Sweat Gear International. The serious, principled challenge from one direction combined well with the exaggerated, satirical challenge from the other direction.

A mock funeral procession outside the Department of Energy dramatizes the dangers of nuclear policy. Washington, DC, April, 1980. *photo Ellen Shub*

If you are going to tell people the truth, you had better make them laugh or they will kill you.

—OSCAR WILDE

Use the power of ritual. Imagine a military general and a politician, slowly and with exaggerated affect, tossing huge bags of money to each other across a wide expanse. Nearby, a support person hands out a fact sheet that tells the rest of the story. Often this kind of non-verbal performance, similar to a ritual, which repeats a simple but visually arresting motion, is more powerful and effective than a full length skit, crammed with facts and figures.

Anchor your story to an image. In an outdoor setting, some people will watch your performance from beginning to end, but others will drop in mid-performance or check you out from afar while passing by. A long plot-driven story doesn't work well for such a shifting audience. To touch everyone, go ahead and tell your story, but anchor it to a strong visual image that people can grasp immediately.

We try to do this with the 10 Musical Chairs (see Chapter 8: Complete Recipes). The whole story happens within a visual scene that conveys the essence of the story.

Publicize by creating a mystery. Activists at the University of Michigan needed a creative way to publicize a ceremony at which they planned to give green-painted bicycles away to the community. They put up stickers all over town that said "The Green Bike is not Locked." They also put up posters which announced that an unusual ceremony would take place at the center of campus at a certain date and time. Nobody knew what this meant or what to expect but everyone talked about it.

In the end over a thousand students showed up to see the performance. By giving the public only half the message, you can sometimes create a curious buzz that very effectively publicizes your action.

Make your group comfortable; Make your target uncomfortable. Control the agenda of the action. Where possible, even write your target into the script. If you have control over the physical setting of the action, arrange chairs, props, audience, entrances and exits, etc. so that participants feel powerful vis a vis the target. Choose settings and actions that are within the experience of participants but outside the experience of the target. Try to surprise your target. Make sure participants are well-rehearsed and prepared.

Involve your Audience. Choral chants, mass sound effects such as roars or murmurs, or simple physical movements are all ways to get an audience participating. Involve the entire audience or involve individual volunteers. Design the plot so that decisions they make, or the volume of their enthusiasm for one option or another, determine the direction of the piece. Try splitting the audience into sections with different roles.

Use Humor to Undermine Authority. Imagine a labor action where the corporate target has to arrest Barney or escort Santa off the property. Authority requires respect and an aura of formality and seriousness. Humor can disrupt this aura and undermine a target's authority.

Describing themselves as "The Conscience of the Art World," the Guerrilla Girls challenge sexism and racism within the nation's museums and galleries through a combustible blend of guerrilla theater, performance art and hard hitting graphics. The Girls remain anonymous, each adopting the name of a great woman artist. Guerrilla Girl with diamonds. *publicity photo 1987*

Use Hidden Identity. Super Barrio (Super Neighborhood Man, in English) is a real-life people's super hero from Mexico. Throughout the 80's and 90's he would show up in mask and cape to block evictions of poor tenants or wrestle evil corporate and government characters at huge outdoor wrestling matches. To this day, no one knows who lies behind the mask, but Super Barrio is a hero to people all over Mexico. You can use hidden identity in a number of ways: to generate mystery, curiosity and interest in the public; to build up a larger than life character; and to set up situations in which your target is unsure how to respond.

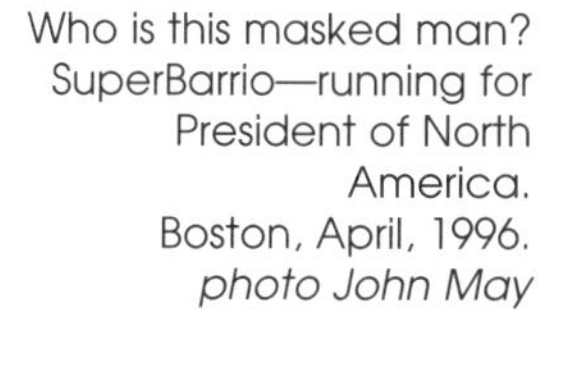

Who is this masked man? SuperBarrio—running for President of North America. Boston, April, 1996. *photo John May*

Use the Aura of Theater. Theater, especially ritual theater with masks and mythical costumes, can inspire awe and command attention. Your target may be unsure how to respond, traffic cops may be unwilling to interrupt you, bystanders might clear out of your way, the curious might follow you. Create and use this aura.

Doing it in the New York City subway. *photo Meryl Levin, Impact Visuals*

Strong opening and closing. Open strong to attract and hold the audience. Close strong to inspire and mobilize.

Shock Carefully and Constructively. In the 1980's campus solidarity groups conducted mock death squad kidnappings during university lectures, hoping to shock people into a deeper awareness of human rights abuses in Central America. Carrying confrontational art directly into people's everyday spaces is a powerful but unilateral tactic, requiring extra responsibility and self-discipline. Respect your audience. Don't shock for the sake of it. Know why you are doing it. Thoughtfully gauge the fine line between shocking and harassing or alienating. Give your audience a way to respond or to have some power in the situation.

Art is a verb.

—Lowery Sims

Stay in Character. In order to preserve the theatrical impact and effect, performers should never break character during direct actions. Where possible, non-performers should handle all supporting tasks, including: outreach, press relations, logistics, set-up and break-down, etc.

Expand your Venues. Perform in places you might not think of: art fairs, county fairs, inside malls, outside malls, wherever there are long lines (sporting events, movie theaters, etc.), silently in libraries, in train or subway stations, etc.

Use Music. Almost any theater action is enhanced by music. Music adds life and energy. It sets the event apart from its surroundings and helps draws a crowd. If you can't find musicians, don't let that stop you—do it yourself. Drumming, clanging, rythmic chanting, etc. are all easy and effective.

PREPARING THE MEAL

No one can tell you how to make a work of art. No one can tell you what is the best creative process for you or your group. You will need to discover that for yourself. (And that's half the joy of the whole thing.) What we can offer you here are some issues to think about, some roles and responsibilities that every creative project needs to cover, and some tools for helping you to invent and solidify your ideas.

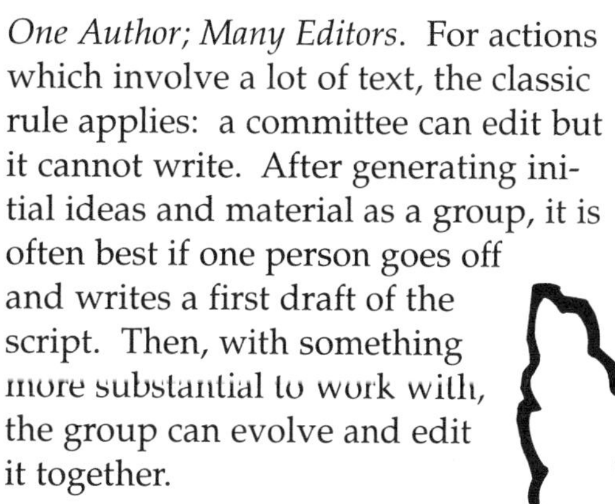

The Creative Process

Just as there are many learning styles, there are also many creative styles. Some people are most at home with words, others with images, feelings, body movement, or rhythm. Some people work more from their head: they begin with an idea, and almost like a mental architect, build up systematically from there. Others like to jump into the middle of things, mess about, see what comes up and take it from there. Some people like to go off on their own, write up a script and bring it back to the group. Others have a more social process; they like to talk and play out an idea with others from scratch.

The creative process can be haphazard, obsessive, sudden, personal, and full of trial and error. Some people are put off or intimidated by this. For others, this is exactly what makes it exciting. Stay open to all these possibilities. Honor the creative process. Experiment. Discover what works for you.

Roles & Responsibilities

Whatever your creative process, here are some ways to give it structure:

Producer. The producer is responsible for overall logistics and organizational matters, including: recruiting participants, scheduling performances and rehearsals, arranging props, publicity, media, etc. Some of these responsibilities can be delegated but one person should coordinate all these aspects of production.

One Author; Many Editors. For actions which involve a lot of text, the classic rule applies: a committee can edit but it cannot write. After generating initial ideas and material as a group, it is often best if one person goes off and writes a first draft of the script. Then, with something more substantial to work with, the group can evolve and edit it together.

Director. It is often necessary to have one person whose artistic judgment is driving and unifying the work. The director has a strong vision of the work and is responsible for turning the idea and script into a whole and coherent performance. Early in the process, participants might want to clearly assign some final decision making authority to this person.

The process of thinking, planning and creating together gives us resonance with one another, with the environment around us, the natural world and all its textures, meaning and mysteries. The process provides clues, links and means of realizing a richer, fairer, finer way of living our lives, in tune with our becoming.

—Joseph Beuys

Scribe. When the group is improvising or brainstorming, ideas, images and pieces of dialogue come up fast and furious. The group might want to designate a scribe to write these down for the whole group to use.

Rehearsals & Theater Games

In a rehearsal we flesh out what the action is, figure out how to do it, and realize how we rely on each other in the doing of it.

A more confrontational action will require more role-playing and contingency planning while a less confrontational action will rely more on exploration and straight rehearsal. To rehearse properly for a confrontational action, someone needs to play the target (the target will play himself during the action). Rehearse with a "hostile" target, a "nice" target and variations in between. Explore the many possible outcomes. Be prepared.

In a rehearsal we don't just learn parts from a script. We invent, improvise, and explore. We figure out who we are, what we're doing and why. By getting into our characters and understanding their motivations, we can create a performance that rings true to ourselves and our audience.

The creation of something new is not accomplished by the intellect but by the play instinct acting from inner necessity. The creative mind plays with the objects it loves.

—C. G. Jung

Theater games and exercises are a great way to do all of the above. They can be used to loosen up, build trust, generate material, or deepen a performer's connection with her character. Countless games and exercises have been developed and you can easily devise your own. *Improvisations for the Theater* by Viola Spolin and Playing Boal: *Theater Games for Actors and Non-Actors* by Augusto Boal (see Chapter 9: Shopping for Fresh Food) alone contain hundreds. Here, are a few which we find useful:

Names, Sounds and Movements. Group gathers in a circle. One volunteer shares some unique movement and sound. Then the whole group repeats it back. This continues around the circle. Instead of a sound, people can say their name in an unusual way. Great as an ice breaker and a wake up.

Fear and Protection. Each person secretly identifies one person as their fear and another person as their protector. Then everyone moves about the space, trying to keep their protector between them and their prey (but nobody knows who anybody else has chosen!). Good for a few laughs and getting people moving around physically.

Mirrors. People pair off and face each other. The first person in the pair leads and the second person tries to follow every move. Then they switch. Then they move together, trying to erase the boundary between leader and follower. Movements should be fluid. Good for focusing the body and building trust.

World. One person begins with a simple action, say, begging for money. Another joins in, walking a dog. A third steps into the scene, trying to hail a cab. A fourth enters as a policeman, trying to move the beggar along. In this way a world is built up. Participants should not know ahead of time what the first person is doing. Good for improvising scenes. Try variations with frozen poses or movement, silence or speaking, etc.

Machine. Someone begins by acting out one part of a larger machine. When someone else decides they understand what kind of machine it is, they join in, and play another part of the machine. This continues until all are participating in the machine as a coordinated whole. Discussion at end of exercise might focus on how people were or weren't able to work together when they had similar and different notions of what the machine was doing. Good for developing group process and teamwork.

Spoof Commercials. In small groups develop 30-60 second spoof TV commercial, for products like "Blando White Bread", "Trickle downers," or "Time Strife books." Good quick way to warm up the verbal and conceptual part of our brains. And lots of fun.

Art for a Fair Economy has also developed several theater games that specifically address issues of social class and economic inequality:

Engines of Inequality. Similar to the "Machine" exercise described above. Participants build machines that illustrate the workings of economic inequality. Participants should be specific and decide up front what economic mechanism to illustrate. Could add two machines together to show economic impact on larger society. Could build another machine that corrects injustices of first machine.

Economic Characters. In this exercise, participants build up characters based on economic archetypes. Everyone is assigned an archetype such as greed, charity, abundance, poverty and sufficiency. Then, milling about in a space together, participants elaborate their character through various stages. Begin with physical, ritual movements. Then add sound and repeating phrases. Then interaction with other characters.

Economic Images. Using a simple chair to represent wealth, each participant composes a series of frozen poses that express key moments in their own economic life. Begin by first exploring all the physical arrangements and relationships you can have with the chair. And end by sharing the story behind one or two of the economic poses with other members in the group. Great for generating powerful images and getting people in touch with their own stories.

Class Spectogram. Arrange yourselves in a line according to where you fall along an economic spectrum and use

Play, fantasy, imaging, free exploration of possibilities: these are the central powers of human beings..

—Brian Swimme

Bosco So in "Dance of the 10 Chairs," a movement piece built upon images drawn from the economic lives of the participants. Somerville, 1996. *photo Laura Wulf*

this as a frame for theatrical and personal exploration.

To find your place in the line, go to where you think you belong and then hash it out with your neighbors. Once everyone is in line, take a moment to look up and down the line and then one at a time, speak about why you put yourself where you did. As people speak, you can reconsider and adjust your location in the line.

photo Ellen Shub

Once the spectogram framework is established, the group can use it to improvise dialogues and scenes.

This exercise can be used to build trust and understanding as well as generate material. But because class issues are often linked to personal and painful feelings, it should be conducted by a sensitive facilitator in an emotionally safe atmosphere. Participants should be given the option of passing whenever they feel uncomfortable.

Ideologies separate us. Dreams and anguish bring us together.

—Eugene Ionesco

Confidence Building

Taking creative risks, performing in public, revealing yourself during rehearsal—all of these things can be scary or embarrassing. Most of us have a deep fear of being seen acting foolish. This is OK. The theater games described above can help people feel more comfortable working together. The exercises below can help build confidence for performing in public.

Pre-performance. Before taking the piece to the public, practice in front of a small, friendly audience who can give you valuable criticisms and suggestions. You may also find it helpful to role-play various audience reactions such as indifference, hostility, and enthusiasm.

Street-speaking. The entire group goes out to a city park or square, with a soap box in hand. Each person takes a turn getting on the soap box and speaking out about a social issue that concerns them, while the rest of the group circles around and listens supportively. This exercise is a nice bridge between a safe and supportive situation and a less predictable public one.

Goofing in public. One really fun way to build your confidence for performing in public is to walk into lamp posts and fall down. Yep, you heard it right. In groups of 3-5, walk along any street or through any mall, and pretend to walk into a pole and fall down—but make it look real. The rest of the group comes quickly over, feigning concern, and helps you to your feet. Continue and repeat. This exercise is great for jarring loose what you allow yourself to do in public.

SERVING THE MEAL

Costume, Props & Set

Although props and costumes will vary greatly with each show, your overriding goal can be usefully summed up as follows: to simply and inexpensively create a striking and unified visual look. To this end a few general suggestions are offered here:

Color. Choose one or two unifying colors for everyone to wear, probably bright but not light.

Hats. Hats are one of the best props: they are strong symbols, easy to manage, visible, and often squishable for transport. Santa hats, bowler hats, hard hats, and baseball caps are all good props and easy to come by.

Where to get stuff. Hunt and peck through scrappy second hand stores for individual items. Or go to big discount or surplus stores to buy cheap, commercial items in bulk (like Santa hats or feather dusters). Or have a set of T-shirts or baseball caps custom printed with the same color and design. Or ask your neighborhood theater if you can borrow some items on a one-time basis. Costume stores are often too expensive, but at party or novelty stores you can get plastic stuff real cheap, especially on the day after Halloween.

Changing costume. Since there is rarely any backstage, it is best to limit costume changes during the show. If necessary, it is best to wear the second costume underneath the first and dramatically strip from one to the other as part of the performance. This is faster, does not distract the audience and reveals the new costume in the best possible way: filled out by a body and immediately in action.

Multiple Functions. To save space and cost, props should have multiple functions. We have used feather dusters as flowers, cheerleader pom-poms, hand-held mustaches, as well as the international symbol of workers in the service economy.

Masks. If you are performing at a distance from your audience, full-face masks combined with large bodily gestures work well.

Backdrops. Backdrops made out of canvas are much easier to transport and handle than those made of wood or cardboard, especially outside in the wind.

For more detailed information on prop making, refer to *Wise Fool Basics* or *The Art of Demonstration* in Chapter 9: Shopping for Fresh Food.

Choosing a Space

The performance space for a direct action is usually at or in front of the target site. For outdoor theater aimed at a passerby audience, you're free to choose almost any space. But choose carefully—going just a few doors down the block or turning the corner can make all the difference. Scope out

The job of the artist is always to deepen the mystery.

—FRANCIS BACON

possible sites prior to the performance.

Backdrop. Try to set up the performance with a plain wall immediately behind. It bounces sound back to the audience, provides a neutral visual background and helps prevent props from being stolen.

Noise. As much as possible, avoid having to compete with other sounds. (Or find a way to integrate them in.) Consider noise from traffic, construction sites, children at play, etc.

Obstruction. Set up in such a way that your audience can gather around without obstructing the street traffic, sidewalk pedestrian flow, or access to a building (unless this is your goal, of course).

Lighting. Be aware that if daytime sun or nighttime streetlight comes from behind you, you will be silhouetted, forcing the audience to squint. Look for light that comes from one side or another.

Weather. If there is wind, it should blow from you to your audience to carry sound. Wind can also wreak havoc with your props—bring weights, rope and tent stakes.

Physical Location. Avoid placing any physical barriers between you and your audience—this causes a feeling of distancing. To be as visible and audible as possible, either you or your audience should be raised up. Ideal is the amphitheater situation with you below and your audience on a series of raised levels. This encloses the sound and makes for a more intimate space. Such arrangements can be found in the city on the side of a mound in a city park, inside a non-working fountain. The other alternative is to raise yourself up, above your audience—on the steps of a public building, or atop a wall, or a line of benches, or...

Create your own Stage. Sometimes it is possible to create your own stage. On one action, the United Brotherhood of Electrical Workers found that the downtown sidewalks outside their target were too narrow, so they rented a flatbed truck, parked it right outside, and did the whole performance on top of it!

I begin with an idea and then it becomes something else.

—Pablo Picasso

Attracting an Audience

There are many ways to attract an audience:

Loud, Large and Colorful:

Barker. A loud "Ladies and gentlemen..." type speech which entices the audience in through sheer volume and promises of a good show.

Music. Loud music, drum roll, trumpet, fanfare. Play it in a way that entices instead of alienating your audience.

Spectacle. A huge prop or puppet. An outrageous costume. Feats of skill: juggling, acrobatics, stilt walking, etc. Doing anything (or nothing) up on a tall ladder.

Subtle, Mysterious, and Intimate:

One-on-one. Engage a single onlooker with a pantomime or antic, then as people stop to watch, do same with another, till a critical mass has built.

Frozen pose. Hold a silent frozen pose that buzzes with tension and expectation.

Set up. Consciously make setting up for the show a show in itself (e.g. physical warm-ups, setting out props, etc.).

Hoax. With a big enough camera and the right attitude, pretend you are the media.

Choose an approach appropriate for the situation. Is your potential audience hanging out leisurely in a park or walking by intent on their destination? Are you performing in a city square where street performers are common or in a shopping mall where a performance is unexpected?

Arranging the Audience and the Performance Area

Once you have drawn an audience it is important to have the performance area clearly marked out. This can be done in a number of ways:

Rope. put a rope on the ground

Chairs. strategically place a few chairs to indicate the front row

Ushering. actually usher initial audience members into place

An audience will naturally form in a circle. However, it is often difficult to perform to a full circle. We recommend that you put your props to the back, establish a front, and have the

...to make the experience of art part of the street scene ...to make the making and the commissioning of art a possibility in any street anywhere, propelled by anyone, thereby bringing art, celebration and activism into a convergent path.

—SUE CLIFFORD & ANGELA KING

Posing as "Pataki's Prisoners," SUNY students protest proposed cuts in education spending. State Capitol Building, Albany NY, March, 1996.
photo Kirk Condyles, Impact Visuals

audience fall in around a one-half or three-quarter circle.

Holding the Audience

We got stuff! At the beginning you may want to do something striking that announces to the audience, "We got stuff! Stick around for more." Similarly, doing something surprising early is a great help because after one surprise, the audience will be wondering what others may be in store.

"She won't sleep with Joe unless he uses a condom." Puppets Against AIDS. *photo Gisele Wulfsohn, Impact Visuals*

Tension. Also key to holding an audience is creating a sense of tension and expectation—if possible, in each part as well as the whole. You want them wondering what's going to happen next? How will it end?

Participation. An audience will also stick around if they are involved. (See suggestions earlier in this chapter.)

Sound and Amplification

When you are performing outdoors it is often hard to be heard. Inevitably, one weighs the advantages of higher volume against the complications of using amplification, including: extra cost, logistical headaches, the emotional distance it can put between you and your audience, the awkwardness of passing a mike back and forth among performers. One compromise solution is to have a narrator read all the lines into a mike while the actors physically perform their parts.

Interruptions

It is in the nature of street theater to risk interruption: hecklers, dogs, toddlers, drunks, police, rain, acts of nature, etc. Some interruptions cause problems, others provide opportunities. Once again, it all depends.

Minor interruptions. Many minor interruptions, such as a dog wandering through the show or a comment from a passing heckler, can be well handled simply by acknowledging it (ideally without stepping out of character) and carrying on.

Major interruptions. With a major interruption—one that threatens to disrupt the whole flow of the show—such as a persistent drunk, a rabid heckler or a downpour, it is better to stop and sort it out.

Respond creatively. An interruption presents a situation that could not be rehearsed and thus may be fascinating to the audience. Where possible, try to approach the interruption creatively. The more open-ended the performance, the easier this will be.

Lengths

The appropriate length for a piece depends on a number of factors. If your audience has come deliberately to see you, then your performance can afford to be longer. If your piece is short and your audience comes and goes, it may make sense to perform continuously, with little or no break between shows. An effective piece can be as short as three minutes. Remember, the audience has no idea how long your piece will take and those who arrive while the piece is under way, don't know how far into the piece they are.

Endings and Outreach

Every action should have a few support people who are not involved in the performance, including:

1) a spokesperson to represent your cause to the press and/or make a pitch to the audience at the close of each show;

2) an information person to give out literature, sign up new members, take donations, etc.; and

3) a photographer or videographer to document the action. (Video cameras can be easily rented from your local cable access station. These stations will also broadcast your uncut footage—just give them the tape.)

Maybe you want to explain your art and maybe you don't. Either way, as a political performer, you're interested in informing, mobilizing and fundraising your audience. And this is often accomplished with a pitch at the end of the piece. However, you don't have to wait until the end of the performance to give out literature. Try not to lose people because the piece ends and you're scurrying around with leaflets as people leave *en masse*.

A little creativity can go a long way. Imagine turning the usual meeting, protest or informational tabling into something unusual, creative, and memorable. Would you do it? Probably. If only you had the time. Well, you've got the time to add these creative twists—some of them take as little as 10 minutes.

Marching band. Liven up a march with a marching band. Identify the musicians among those who are already coming and make sure they bring their instruments (drums, trumpets, bagpipes, flutes, etc.). Let them figure out what to play and how to play together when they arrive.

Write a song. Take a popular tune that everyone knows and rewrite the lyrics to address your issue. (You'd be surprised how little time this takes.) Copy and hand out at event. Have one person lead the group. Everyone will join in and have fun at the target's expense.

If you want musical accompaniment but don't have your own musicians, check out your local record store for an "extended mix" dance tape which contains a version of the song with instruments alone. Pop the tape in the boom box and sing your own lyrics, Karaoke style.

Another helpful tool for prospective song-writers is a rhyming dictionary. There is a pocket edition is available for $3.

One person theater. Even the quickest and dirtiest theater can create a strong photo-op for an outdoor event. All you need is one person dressed in character, or one person on stilts with an appropriate hat or mask. Think about what setting to place them in (usually in front of the target, if there is one) to get the event's message across with a single snapshot. If you have a little more time, add another character—now you can portray a relationship.

"Tell Ron (Reagan) it Won't Play." Burma Shave signs in action, Peoria, IL. *photo courtesy of Midwest Academy*

Burma Shave Signs. Instead of putting your whole slogan on one sign, spread it out across a series of signs, putting one word or one letter on each sign. Then you can have a series of people, each holding one part of the slogan, positioned along a road or pedestrian flow. Passing motorists as well as the media, may find this visually interesting. It also has a nice touch of united effort. (In a similar way, you can set up a series of rhyming slogans, one on each sign, staggered down the road.)

Creative leafleting. Instead of straightforward leafleting, do something creative: do it with one person on another's shoulders; do it in a simple costume; hand out something symbolic with the leaflet.

Creative meetings. Combine the meeting with a potluck. Plan to go out together after the meeting and have fun (this will also provide strong incentive to end on time). Do something at the beginning of the meeting to laugh, and get everybody's juices flowing. In the popular movement in El Salvador there is a tradition of breaking up meetings with little energetic exercises called "dinamicas." In one of them, everyone stamped their foot three times, spun round, and said, "Yaaaaaaah!" Come up with new ones every meeting. Or try using one of the theater games suggested in Chapter 3: Soup to Nuts.

Creative fundraisers. Make it fun for people to give away their money. Use your imagination. At one event an activist group created various installations that mocked fundraising technologies: a clothesline with trousers hanging from it (put your donation in one of the pockets); an ATM machine that dispensed poetry fragments instead of receipts; a huge direct mail letter and envelope; and a desk with a tape recorder and a hilarious message buffooning a computer automated telemarketer.

Creative parties. Come up with an engaging theme, eye-catching flyer and some fun interactive social activities: an economic fortune telling booth, a poetry wall, a piñata of the political figure you love to hate—whatever your imagination can dream up. Have a media room with videos and printed information. Have the activities off to the side, so that people can do them when and as they see fit and it doesn't require the whole party to switch gears.

When the artist is alive in any person, whatever his kind of work may be, he becomes an inventive, searching, daring, self-expressive creature. He becomes interesting to other people. He disturbs, upsets, enlightens, and opens ways for a better understanding. Where those who are not artists are trying to close the book, he opens it and show there are still more pages possible.

—Robert Henri,
The Art Spirit

Here is a sampling of creative action ideas from around the country. Help yourself. Spice to taste. Play with your food.

Popular Theater Performances

War of the Worlds, Part II. A skit based on Orson Welles' famous 1930's-era radio play—but instead of Martians, trans-national corporations take over the Earth. Samples: "They're hideous to behold; cold and calculating, their tentacles reaching out everywhere... can nothing stop them...?" "Their dark ships hovering over government buildings, their deadly lasers striking out without warning, aaaarrrrrggg, oh my God! They've burned a Mickey Mouse symbol into the White House lawn..."

Mobile Identity. A skit set in a beauty salon. Instead of getting a nose job or a perm, the customer receives a full class identity makeover.

The Price is Wrong. A skit that uses a spoof of the TV-game show to criticize the illogical and imbalanced prices of different kinds of labor and items ($500 Pentagon toilet seats, unpaid child rearing, invisibly subsidized gasoline, excessive corporate salaries, etc.)

Family Feud. Uses the same format as the popular TV-game show, but the two "families" are Boss and Union. The Boss family is played by a bunch of bad-guy characters, while the Union family is played by the audience, with a group of 3-6 coming up out of the audience for each new round. As in the TV show, the game answers are based on a questionnaire circulated to the whole audience prior to the show, and might include: "Name something you call your boss, when he's not around," and "Name something that would improve your workplace." (For a copy of the entire script, contact: Julie McCall, 739 Rock Creek Church Road N.W., Washington, D.C. 20010 • 202/882-0360.)

One-Minute Downsizer. A skit that plays off of the popular "one-minute manager" series of business self-help books.

Auction America. An auction in which various states and cities vie to have a new stadium or factory relocate to their area. The bidding escalates to absurd levels as mayors and governors try to out bid each other, promising more and more tax-breaks, subsidies and give-aways (not to mention the key to the city, all firstborns with brown eyes, etc.) to the greedy corporation.

Sound Bites from History. A skit that presents a sequence of historical figures (e.g. Carnegie, Jefferson, Plato, Rousseau, etc.) who have made surprisingly radical and provocative statements about wealth. Could take the form of either a rogues' gallery, a press conference, or a single actor cycling through a quick succession of prop changes.

Robin Hood: Folk Hero or Leach on Society?. A skit featuring Robin Hood, depressed and out of place in 1990's America. Scenes might include break-up with Maid Marian, therapy session, talk show. Samples: "Nobody understands my work anymore." "These days you just can't make a living stealing from the rich and giving to the poor..."

Life with the Slabinnac Cimonoce. A skit in which a bewildered extra-terrestrial anthropologist documents (into his micro-cassette recorder) the economic mores, arrangements and rituals of the contemporary human scene. (p.s. that's "Economic Cannibals" spelled backwards.)

Sweatshop Fashion Show. A performance which uses a fashion show format, complete with runway and models, to expose the sweatshops behind the designer labels.

A Prison for Every Occasion. A skit that portrays how economic apartheid is putting us all in prison. Show a maximum security cell and a posh, gated community (with private security, alarm system, etc.). Maybe show both simultaneously, splitting the stage between them.

Economics 101: The Lost Data. A skit in which an economics professor

Human salvation lies in the hands of the creatively maladjusted.

—Martin Luther King

What grabs people's attention and stay in their minds is usually not an argument or a fact but an image or a story.

—Timothy Saasta

"I've taken up art."

"Why?"

"Well, since the opposite of art is insensibility, a life that is mute, formless, unexpressed, emptily repetitive, a vacuous routine with failure of creativity and..."

"Good grief! Chuck me some clay!"

—HARGREAVES, HAYSEEDS CARTOON STRIP

When people laugh, their brains temporarily open and a few ideas can be nailed in before they close again.

—MOLIERE

stands at a podium laying out a cut and dried economic analysis while, in a different "zone", those made invisible by his data (undocumented workers, the structurally unemployed, forests and rivers, etc.), drift and toil and mutter. At intervals, the "invisibles" raise their voice above the drone of data and tell their story. (Instead of a professor, one could use an "average guy or gal" sitting at the kitchen table, reading the business section of the newspaper out loud).

Taboo. A skit featuring two characters who talk about everything in their lives except class. They get heavy and personal into all kinds of charged topics and intimate sharing (politics, sexuality, family histories of alcoholism and abuse, etc.) but each time they come close to sharing their class background or current income, etc. they deftly move off topic. Timing, subtlety, and inference are important here. Could be quite funny and on target but might require a fair amount of rehearsal effort to get it just right.

Inequality Olympics. A framework for a series of carnival and sporting-event spoofs that dramatize how the "rules" of the economic "game" are rigged against the average American. In addition to the Rat Race (described in depth in Chapter 8: Complete Recipes), other components might include:

Born on Third Base and Thought They Hit a Triple. Absurd baseball game that demonstrates how the very wealthy, while claiming to have earned their wealth the hard way, often start way ahead of the game. Some wealthy players would begin on third base, etc. Could use recent research done by United for a Fair Economy on the Forbes 400 (see Appendix).

Two Wage Earner Relay Race. A harried couple run alternating laps, passing their baby (doll) back and forth as if it were a baton, never getting to spend quality time together. This skit could be ongoing, either in the background of other skits or in the interludes between them, with a rare spoken line once in a while to draw back the audience's attention. Skit could also be partly performed in aisles of theater.

Minimum Wage Limbo. Corporate ringmaster keeps bringing down the limbo bar as wages get more and more depressed. Maybe things get so bad that only child labor can make it through and finally only a corpse can be dragged under the bar. A little scrolled-out banner reading "corporate profits" might fill the vertical space between where the bar began and where it ends.

Budget Balancing Act. A circus act spoof in which the federal budget gets balanced on the backs of the poor with tax cuts on one side of the scale and service cuts on the other, etc.

Economic Marathon. A hyped-up, horse-racing style announcer gives blow-by-blow political and economic history while runners representing various economic groups run around a circuit, jockeying for advantage, falling forward or racing ahead as events affect them.

Credit Card Pole Vault. Each time you charge it the pole gets higher—but how else can you establish a credit rating and stay ahead of stagnating wages.

Street Theater Actions

10 Chairs on the Subway & 10 Chairs on a Park Bench. Perform a version of the 10 Chairs (see Chapter 8: Complete Recipes) on the subway or a park bench. Use 10 adjacent subway seats (the old Red Line trains in Boston are set up this way—maybe other subways in other cities are as well). Get on at the end of the line. Maybe perform a silent version. Hand out leaflets. Generate media intrigue.

10 Chairs as an "Artistic Vigil". Perform a tableau of the 10 chairs that is like a vigil but with the power of a monument: a stark, silent, and solemn portrayal of economic inequity—part human sculpture, part ritual and part witness to injustice. Perform outside appropriate target, such as Federal Reserve Building, etc. Perform for an hour every day for a series of days.

Tara Mooney performs "Dance of the 10 Chairs," a movement piece originally conceived of as an "artistic vigil." Boston, 1996. *photo Mike Massey*

Corporate Soup Kitchen. A soup kitchen that instead of serving soup and rice and bread to the needy, serves subsidies, tax cuts, and contracts to the greedy. Great vehicle for educating around corporate welfare. The Homeless Action Committee in Ann Arbor, MI put this on as a quick and dirty media stunt. A more ambitious and artsy version might be an ongoing outdoor installation-performance. Maybe set it up outside a shelter or welfare office to drive the point home. Could also work as a simple indoor theater skit.

Xmas Carols for the Rest of Us. Take traditional Christmas carols and rework them to carry a critical message. Then go caroling around town or in front of politically charged sites. A few that we came up with: "Deck the Malls," "Come All Ye Paupers," "Violent Night" (about domestic violence). The possibilities are endless and it is great fun. You could also try and air them on local radio.

Guerrilla Theater Actions

Noh Business as Usual. A group of 3-7 people, in full matching corporate gear, go to a busy financial district setting and walk extremely slowly and with intense concentration, capturing the gestures of a corporate rush hour walk. Maybe one person holds a sign which asks, "What's the hurry?" ("Noh" is a traditional Japanese theater style.)

Cardboard Desires (version 1). Two people stand around with sandwich boards on a busy rush-hour street corner, at a distance from each other, eyeing each other suspiciously. One is a down and out worker whose sign says "will work for food" or some such. The other is dressed as a CEO, with sign "will work for $3 million, stock options, etc."

"I've been robbed...!". On a street corner, person starts yelling "I've been robbed, I've been robbed!" When people gather, she transitions to address them with "...and so, ladies and gentleman, have you: by the very, very wealthiest among us...not at gun point, not with a knife, but legally, etc." Use your wits and caution here, for obvious reasons. A classic street action used by IWW labor activists in the 1910's.

People that are really very weird can get into sensitive positions and have a tremendous impact on history.

—Dan Quayle

Invisible Theater Actions

Cardboard Desires (version 2). A series of performers slump against a building wall at various intervals along a sidewalk, looking homeless and holding hand scrawled cardboard signs with statements that range from the outraged to the absurd. Maybe each performer has a line for passersby as well. Maybe performance is developed in conjunction with organized homeless groups and built around a real homeless person already there who is willing to participate.

Virtual Preacher. A performer impersonates a wild-eyed, fire and brimstone street preacher but instead of the usual evangelical rant, he speaks radical truths about the society and the economy. He should, however, retain the evangelical style and his statements should include moral allegory, chapter and verse quotations, etc. Liberation theology sources might provide ideas for content and selected Bible passages.

Appearance of Class. Performers, dressed to represent different class positions, enter social spaces (such as stores, restaurants and the lobbies of office buildings) and build invisible theater scenes around the different reactions they might provoke.

Media Stunts

Welcome to America. At any international airport, greet tourists with a warning: "The United States is the most economically unequal of all industrialized nations and on top of that inequality is growing faster than in any other industrialized nation." Maybe one performer dresses up rich, the other poor and hold signs (as if for chauffeur service) "rich" and "poor."

In Bed with Big Business: Put two performers, representing corporations and government, into a bed and roll it up the steps of the legislature. Continue performance all day. When a similar stunt was pulled by activists in Arizona, they vowed to remain until "government gets out of bed" with the corporations. TV stations gave live updates from the bed.

Santa Claus: Childhood Fable or Friend of Corporate Interests? Use a Santa figure to dramatize how corporations get most of the government gifts. Maybe use different sized stockings or gifts to visually demonstrate unequal shares.

In 1983 a big fight was brewing at the University of Michigan. Student peace groups were holding vigils and sit-ins, trying to ban military research from campus. Scientists were claiming, with considerable success, that their work was civilian in nature. One group of students decided it was time to try a different approach.

They disguised themselves in dark sunglasses, Walkman™ head sets, and white lab coats. Claiming to be members of the Nuclear Saints of America, a right-wing religious cult, they took over a military research lab.

Each student brought along their own military research project (knitting a nose cone warmer in the school colors, for example) and refused to leave the lab until they got some research done. Mistaking the action for a show of support, the lead scientist enthusiastically joined in a religious ceremony in which Atomic Fire Ball candy was given out as communion.

He eventually realized his mistake, but it was too late. The story, complete with telling photos, was all over the next morning's papers.

Our nation is facing dangerous levels of economic inequality. In the last twenty years, the rich have gotten richer and are pulling away from everyone else.

During the 1980's, our jobs and the wealth of our communities were treated like gambling casinos—and ordinary people lost. This is why many of our lives are more insecure, why we are working longer hours with less security, and why people at the bottom are getting scapegoated.

The wealthy and powerful have developed numerous ways of maintaining this situation (dominating the media, changing government tax rules, etc.) and diverting Americans' attention away from these essential concerns.

WHAT IS THE CURRENT INEQUALITY SITUATION?

Income - During the period from 1979 until the present, the growth in income has disproportionately flowed to the top. The bottom 60% of the population actually saw their real income decrease in constant dollars. The next 20% saw modest gains. The top twenty percent saw their income increase 18%. The wealthiest one percent saw their incomes explode over 110%.

Wealth - In 1976, the wealthiest one percent of Americans owned 19% of all the private material wealth in the U.S. Today, they own over 40% of all wealth. They now own more wealth than the bottom 92% of the U.S. population combined.

The shift in the ownership of income and wealth—and the changing nature of work—will hit the next generation particularly hard. Many young people who grew up in middle class families will never have a standard of living approaching their parents—and will increasingly be dependent on their parents' "equity" to help them build any security. Lower income youth face a lifetime of economic insecurity.

Unless we change our direction we are likely to end up where we are headed.

—Old Chinese Proverb

HOW DID THIS HAPPEN?
These dire circumstances were not the result of sun spots. They are the outcome of specific policy choices, made by human beings. A white "overclass," as writer Michael Lind describes our nation's wealth and power elite, has succeeded in changing the political rules to shift the tax burden off corporations and the wealthy onto the middle and working class and reward asset holders at the expense of wage earners.

The economic security of the bottom two hundred million people in the U.S. has been sacrificed to increase the wealth of the richest two million.

At the same time, this overclass has succeeded in capitalizing on divisions in multi-cultural America by race, gender and age—unleashing a wave of "regressive populism."

As economic insecurity climbs up the economic ladder, reaching into formerly secure middle class homes, resentment and anger grows. Instead of directing these sentiments toward concentrated wealth and unbridled corporate power, people are looking down the economic ladder, scapegoating those less privileged than themselves.

WHY HAS WEALTH SHIFTED IN RECENT YEARS?
Growing inequality in the U.S. is the result of a growing imbalance of power between powerful money interests and everyone else. The voice and perspective of wealthy individuals and corporations has become dominant—while the concerns of ordinary working Americans have been lost.

Labor unions, which have historically have given working people's concerns a voice and power, have been dramatically weakened over the last forty years. In the 1950s, over 33% of the US workforce was unionized. Today, less than 15% of workers are protected by a union.

This imbalance of power has lead to some dramatic changes in the rules governing our global economy. These "rule changes" include changes in global trade, tax laws, compensation and more.

A. Changes in Trade Rules and Globalization
U.S. multi-national corporations have been working to change the rules governing global trade—to pit U.S. workers against workers in countries lacking human rights, environmental protections and the right to organize unions. This has the effect of driving down wages in the U.S. and keeping everyone in the planet in a state of economic insecurity.

Free trade agreements would be less reprehensible if they were also "fair

Jesus saves, but he couldn't on my wages.

—GRAFFITO

trade" agreements, guaranteeing minimal environmental standards and fair labor practices in countries with which we trade.

B. Changes in Tax Rules

During the 1950s, government tax and spending policies worked to build the commonwealth of this country and gave most Americans more access to affordable education, home ownership, and decent jobs.

Through Federal programs such as GI Bill and low interest mortgages, all classes shared together the fruits of the post-World War II growth, with each segment of society seeing income gains of over 100% between 1950 and 1975. The biggest leap went to the bottom one-fifth of the population, whose income grew 138% during these years.

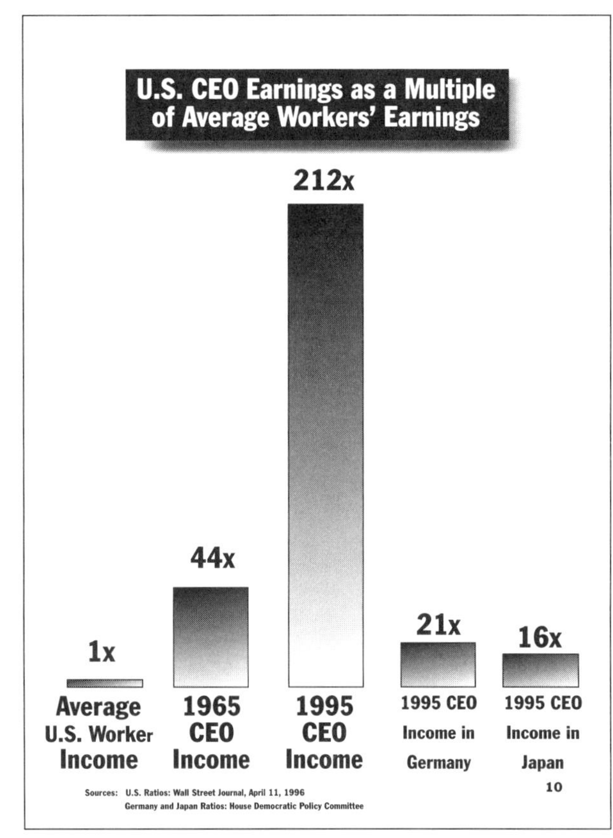

During the Reagan-Bush years, the emphasis of tax policy was to promote "trickle down" economics under the theory that cutting taxes on the rich (and raising them on everyone else) would create more wealth in society for all. The theory was that if the rich kept more of "their" wealth they would invest it which would grow the economy and we would all benefit.

Taxes on the wealthy were cut from a top rate of 68% in 1980s to 28% by 1988. The share of federal tax revenue paid by corporations has dropped from 33 cents of every dollar collected in 1953 to less than 10 cents today. Very little of this wealth trickled down, however. Instead, we witnessed the single greatest upward redistribution of wealth in our nation's history.

C. The Widening Wage Gap: Overpaid Bosses and Underpaid Workers

The gap between highest and lowest paid workers in the United States has dramatically widened. In 1974, the ratio between highest and lowest paid workers was 41 to one. Today, the gap has widened to over 200 to one. CEOs like Thomas Frist of Hospital Corporation of America got paid over $127 million in 1992, or roughly $61,000 an hour or $16 a second.

Workers for their part have taken it on the chin. Corporations have not only been paying their workers less, but have been downsizing at a rapid pace. According to Business Week, worker layoffs increased 39% between 1990 and 1995. All of this has forced average Americans to ask what happened to their Dream.

The National Debt is an Inequality Engine

One perverse result of the changing tax and spending rules is that our national debt redistributes wealth from working people to wealthy bond-holders. Between 1980 and 1992, our national public debt grew from less than one trillion to almost five trillion dollars. For every six dollars the government spent during the 1980s, it only collected five dollars.

The gap was filled by borrowing funds from the wealthy at home and abroad. About a fifth of our $5 trillion debt is owed to foreign interests. But most is owed to the top 5% of U.S. asset owners. The wealthy bond-owners, holding funds that in previous years might have been taxed, lend money, at interest, to the rest of us. This 14 cents on every tax dollar which we pay just in interest on the debt is a transfer payment to the wealthy.

This does not mean public borrowing is inherently bad. Federal deficit spending is helpful to an economy in recession and when unemployment is high. The problem with the debt build-up of the 1980s was that the money wasn't invested productively for the future. Instead, money was borrowed to pay for tax breaks for the rich, the savings and loan bailout, and military hardware. Brutal cuts in social programs for the poor did not reduce the size of annual deficits. The public at large is being asked to pay the bill for a wild speculation binge and tax cut benefiting the wealthy.

Speculation Binges

Another perverse result of these changes is the increase of speculation in our economy. Instead of wealth trickling down, it gushed to the top. This process unleashed a speculative frenzy that bankrupted our savings and loan industry, drove our jobs into the ground or overseas, and destabilized our economy.

Real estate speculation during the 1980s was fueled by provisions in the tax code that encouraged the rapid turnover of rental housing. As a result, a majority of people now suffer from high rents, unattainable home ownership or hefty mortgages that require two incomes to support. Homelessness has soared.

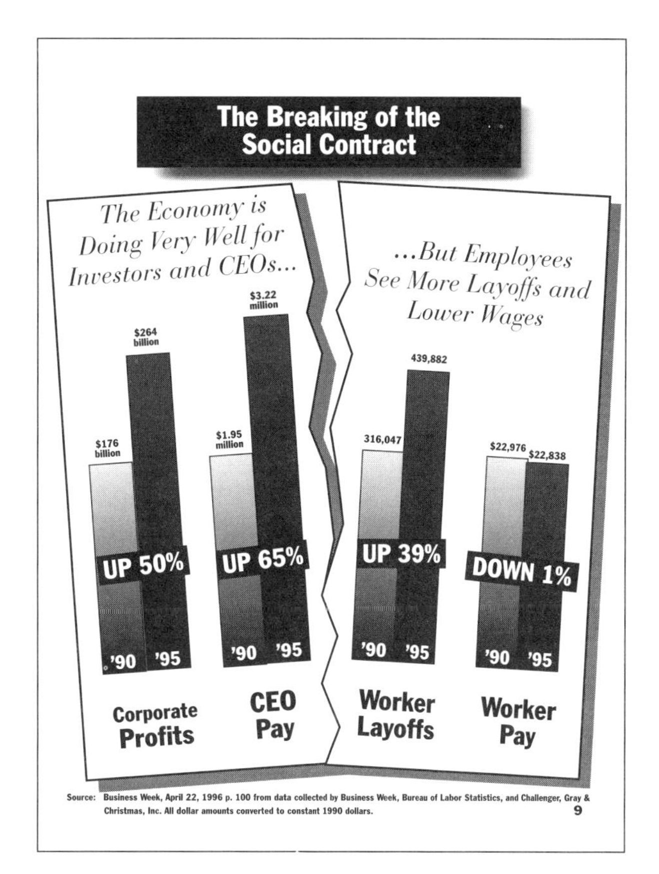

U.S.-based multi-national corporations, using provisions of the tax code which they wrote and lobbied for, have taken their companies, jobs and tax payments overseas.

The great American Unease is fundamentally rooted in the changing nature of work. Economist Wallace

All amassing of wealth or hoarding of wealth above and beyond one's legitimate needs is theft. There would be no occasion for theft and no thieves if there was wise regulation of wealth and social justice.

—M. K. GANDHI

Where wealth is centralized, the people are dispersed. Where wealth is distributed, the people are brought together.

—CONFUCIUS

Peterson points out that three out of four U.S. workers have experienced a decline in their standard of living: either a drop in purchasing power, a loss of benefits, or a change in job security. More and more people have the experience of being "temped," "adjuncted" or "downsized."

FINDING SOLUTIONS, NOT SCAPEGOATS

At the same time as wealth has been propelled from our pockets into the vaults of the wealthy, we have been told to blame ourselves or others for our insecurity and inability to prosper. We are told that welfare recipients and new immigrants are the causes of our growing tax burden and economic insecurity.

Reprinted with special permission of King Features Syndicate ©

But we need solutions, not scapegoats. We need to build real economic security, not casinos, jails, and temp jobs. We need to stop waiting for the wealth to trickle down. We need to build an economy that is environmentally sustainable, with jobs that strengthen all our communities.

Adding your voice, talents and skills to the debate is essential. New creative ideas and action have to be developed. The media cannot speak for us, nor can corporate power. But we allow them to when we remain silent.

THE ROAD AHEAD AND YOUR PART

This is the present situation. Our future does not have to follow that same path. There are many in Congress, both Democrat and Republican, primed to either maintain the status quo or push for even stronger reactionary policies. If citizens choose not to stand up and vocally express their opinions, we could all be in for another round of "trickle down" economics and hand outs to the wealthy.

ENOUGH IS ENOUGH!

How much of our nation's wealth should be in the hands of so few? Should we wait until the wealthiest one percent have over half of our nation's wealth to declare the wealth gap a problem?

The current situation is not economically or socially sustainable. Too much polarization in society creates insecurity for everyone, even the wealthy. Corporate speculation and global domination without accountability hurts people at home and abroad.

WHAT WILL ADDRESS INEQUALITY?

Proposals that will truly address economic inequality are currently not on the political radar screen. In fact, things seem to be moving in the opposite direction toward policy ideas which will worsen inequality.

What should we do? We need to take a longer view—ten to twenty years. It has taken a long time for the overclass to get so much power. It will take time for us to organize to get it back. We need to think strategically about what efforts today will help us build a broader movement tomorrow that will address the root causes of inequality.

We need to build a progressive political, social and cultural movement to focus on beginning to close the income and wealth gap. These include:

Stop Initiatives That Will Worsen Inequality. Fight Congressional proposals for a flat tax, more capital gains tax cuts and other tax loopholes, punitive welfare reform and other proposals that will only worsen the growing divide in our nation.

Link Wages To CEO Salaries. Work for a livable wage by increasing the hourly minimum wage and limiting the deductibility of excessive salaries. The Income-Equity Act would raise the minimum wage two dollars and deny corporations the right to deduct salaries that exceed 25 times the lowest paid worker in a firm.

Campaign Finance Reform. Remove the excessive influence of big money in politics through far-reaching campaign finance reform. Ban gifts from corporations and finance elections publicly with spending caps for media.

Eliminate Corporate Welfare. Cut the hundreds of billions in subsidies and unproductive loopholes that flow to America's wealthiest individuals and corporations. We estimate there is over $200 billion a year that could be cut.

Corporate Taxation. Institute a two-tier corporate taxation system that rewards socially responsible companies with lower taxes. Companies that pay a living wage, maintain a reasonable ratio between top and bottom workers, don't pollute and are good citizens in the communities where they operate would qualify for a lower tax rate. Irresponsible companies would be subject to a higher tax rate and the taxes would be used to clean up the problems they created.

Increase the Voice of Working People. Remove barriers to free, democratic union elections and the formation of worker centers. Strengthen the voice and power of people who work for a living—as a check against the power of concentrated wealth and corporations.

A little rebellion now and then is a good thing.

—THOMAS JEFFERSON

As an organizer I start from where the world is, as it is, not as I would like it to be. That we accept the world as it is does not in any sense weaken our desire to change it into what we believe it should be–it is necessary to begin where the world is if we are going to change it to what we think it should be.

—SAUL ALINSKY

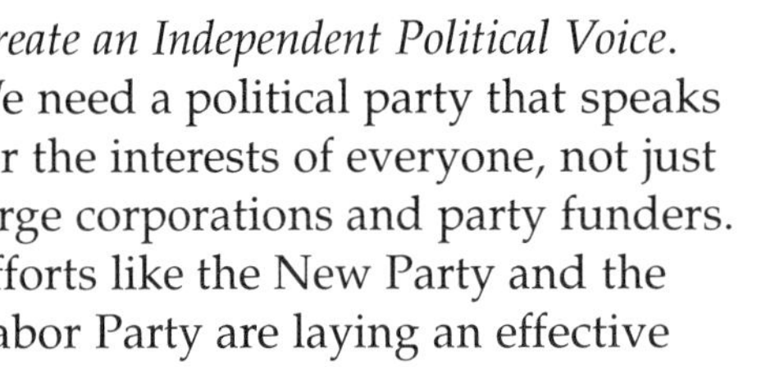

Create an Independent Political Voice. We need a political party that speaks for the interests of everyone, not just large corporations and party funders. Efforts like the New Party and the Labor Party are laying an effective groundwork for an independent political voice. Reforming our election system to allow proportional representation and fusion candidates (candidates that run simultaneously on more that one party ticket) will revitalize our democracy.

"Insurance should make us healthy, not wealthy." Garment workers come out for universal health care, Boston, June, 1991.
photo Ellen Shub

If we work on campaigns like these, we might in the future be able to propose:

Boost the Top Tax Rate. Raise the top tax bracket on the wealthiest one percent of households back to its pre-1980 levels of about 60%. Aim to get the "effective rate" that the wealthy pay closer to 25%.

Close the Wage Gap with a Maximum Wage. Institute a 100% tax rate on wages that exceed a ratio of 25 times the minimum wage. This would create tremendous pressure to raise the minimum wage: for each $1.00 the minimum wage is raised, the wealthy would keep $25.

Institute Wealth Taxation. Many European countries tax accumulated assets above a certain threshold. A modest US wealth tax would raise an additional $40 billion a year in revenue, restore greater progressivity to the federal tax code, and barely make a dent in the lifestyles of the rich.

Get Democratic Control Over Corporations. Reassert democratic control over the chartering of corporations in order to make them more accountable to the communities that they operate within.

Things You Can Do Today...
Join United for a Fair Economy. Membership is only $25, includes a quarterly subscription to the newsletter, "Too Much," and links you to a network of creative cultural organizing and political activism.

Educate. Educate yourself and friends on the depth of the inequality issue.

Link up. Forge alliances with other cultural activists to raise consciousness about this issue in your community.

In 1990, 1700 steelworkers in Ravenswood, WV were locked out of the factory where they had worked for years. Union organizers traced control of the plant back to Mark Rich, a multi-billionaire commodities trader wanted by the US government for tax evasion, and currently hiding out in Zug, Switzerland. Organizers created several huge puppets, including one of Mark Rich himself as well as a 20ft tall puppet of Mother Jones, the gutsy 19th century union activist.

With the puppets in tow, activists flew to Switzerland and picketed his office. Then they took the show on the road, picketing his trading companies in the Netherlands, the UK, Venezuela, Romania, and Czechoslovakia. Wherever Mark Rich did business, the puppets were there. Media on three continents covered the controversy. Eventually he backed down, the plant was re-opened and workers got their contract. Who says you can't do international guerrilla theater?

THE CHALLENGE
Talking about class and inequality in America is tricky. Sharing personal information about one's income, rent, debt, tax payments, etc. is often taboo. Democracy and capitalism are fused together in the minds of many people who then perceive any questioning of economic structures as an attack on democratic government.

Without a framework that makes the underlying factors visible, people turn to scapegoats, blaming immigrants, welfare moms, and the Japanese for their economic difficulties. But in spite of these obstacles, people all over the country are "talking equality."

Our challenge is to understand "the American Palate"—how we think, feel, listen, dream, and bitch about these issues—and then to find the right language to respond creatively and positively. This chapter offers some analysis, approaches and strategies for doing just this.

APPROACHES
Some general approaches for "talking equality."

Reclaim and reinterpret the symbols and mythology of America
We can't let the rich and corporations capture the symbols that have resonance in our culture. The flag, the American Dream, patriotism, the family, and the notions of basic fairness and prosperity for all are all part of popular and progressive traditions. Many of the principles and values linked to these symbols are positive and the public strongly identifies with them. We cannot afford to treat them

as somehow tainted by right wing ideology. Let's take our cue from a button from the 80's which read, "Peace is Patriotic" and the words of Martin Luther King, "I have a dream. It's part of the American Dream."

Redefine what key words mean
Choosing our own names, whether that is *African-American*, *working class*, or *dyke*, is an important part of defining who we are. Likewise, finding the right words for an issue is critical to its call upon hearts and minds. Using the term "corporate welfare" to describe government subsidies to corporations gave this movement a lot of ideological leverage. Abbie Hoffman used to say, "A 'terrorist' is someone who doesn't have a plane to drop his bombs from," reminding us that the most powerful definitions often rest on invisible assumptions.

Fit your message to your audience
Everyone is affected by economic inequality—but often in quite different ways, both direct and indirect. We need to be sensitive to these differences. Make it easy for each constituency to connect with the issue in ways that are meaningful to them.

Use economic inequality as an "umbrella" and a "wedge"
Economic inequality contributes to many other social ills: racism, domestic violence, etc. In your work try to use inequality as an "umbrella issue" that can unite disparate progressive causes. You can also try to use it as a progressive "wedge issue" that can redefine the debate and split the conservative cultural bloc. Conservative wedge issues such as welfare, anti-immigration, reproductive rights, school prayer, gay rights, etc. have divided the majority of low and moderate income citizens. Inequality and economic insecurity can bring these majorities back together. Jobs are becoming more important than gun control.

Honor the complexities of class
Social class is complicated. It is often unclear where and on what basis to draw the line between have's and have not's: income? wealth? education? status? power? An individual's class background (what class they came from), class position (what class they're in) and class identity (what class they feel part of or aspire to be part of) can all be different. Race, gender, age, (dis)ability, and sexual orientation all play a role in the equation. In our work we need to be sensitive to these complexities.

Words are a form of action, capable of influencing change.

—Ingrid Bengis

Eat the rich?
In the making of any popular art work around issues of wealth, sooner or later one question always comes up, whether it's spoken out loud or not: "How to portray the wealthy?" Your choices span everything from a grotesque caricature of an unredeemably evil enemy of the people to a complex and conflicted individual who is just like the rest of us, except for a few extra zeros on his or her bank statement. While different artists and art forms will gravitate to one end of the spectrum or another, we offer the following (conflicting) points for your consideration:

The law in its majestic equality forbids the rich as well as the poor to sleep under bridges, to beg in the streets and to steal bread.

—Anatole France

- Emphasize that inequality undermines everyone's security, even the security of the wealthy.
- Distinguish between responsible wealth and predatory wealth. (Remember, we should be trying to differentiate the wealthy along the lines of conscience and a larger sense of self-interest.)
- Don't worry so much about turning off the wealthy (they have the resources to defend themselves)—but definitely worry about turning off those who sympathize with the wealthy.
- Where possible, honor complexity and avoid cardboard caricature. It is often too easy to just demonize the wealthy. Complexity is more true to life, more interesting and often more believable.
- On the other hand, sometimes you need to forgo subtlety in order to focus people's real and deserved anger on the proper target.
- We should approach this question in the spirit of non-violence. It is important to claim the moral high ground and speak out against stereotyping and scapegoating of any kind.

MYTHS AND COUNTER-STRATEGIES

Here we survey some of the deep cultural myths that shape our views around issues of economic inequality and suggest strategies for challenging them.

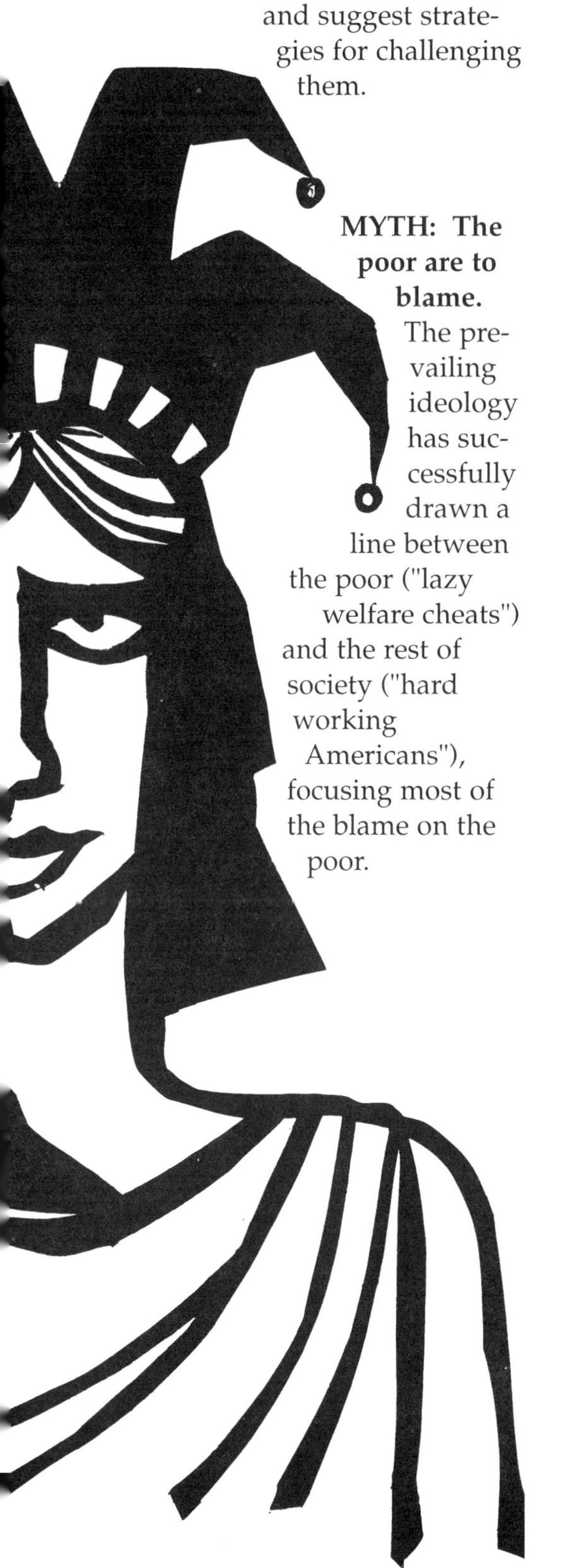

MYTH: The poor are to blame.
The prevailing ideology has successfully drawn a line between the poor ("lazy welfare cheats") and the rest of society ("hard working Americans"), focusing most of the blame on the poor.

COUNTER-STRATEGY: Shift blame from the poor to corporations and the rich
Re-focus attention on the corporations and the super-rich (the top 1%) and the fact that the rest of us have far more in common with one another than any of us have with the very wealthy. Portray welfare moms and other targets of scapegoating in a positive and deeply human light.

****

MYTH: Inequality is disconnected from public policy.
The prevailing ideology claims that the economy is a "free" market, operating by its own natural and non-political logic, with opportunity available more or less equally to all. There is a strong feeling that "the wealthy worked to deserve their wealth."

COUNTER-STRATEGY: Talk about "rule changes"
To speak about fairness and the economy, it is helpful to use a game metaphor. One can then speak of major shifts in the economy as "changes in the rules of the game." Extending the metaphor, one can describe fairness as a "level playing field" or "playing by the rules" and unfairness as "a rigged race."

This characterization helps us to reframe the debate as a "social" or "structural" problem and not as a problem with "individuals." Specifically, it helps us make a more systematic attack on "the rules that create inequality" instead of a more personal (and controversial) attack on "the wealthy individuals who benefit". It also opens the door to hope and action: if the wealthy changed the rules for their own benefit, we also can change them—this time to benefit the majority.

"Our economic system is best described as welfare for the rich and free enterprise for the poor."

—CHARLES ABRAMS, CITY PLANNER

One can also build a host of effective slogans, cartoons or theater pieces around spoofs of sporting events and game shows. An audience immediately gets what is wrong when shown a game with absurd rules or crooked players. It is a powerful way to demonstrate obvious unfairness.

The metaphor is rich in other ways as well: scores and distances allow one to bring in numbers, referees can represent rule-makers or arbiters or enforcers, announcers give the media spin, etc.

(For some great examples of sporting event spoofs, see the "Inequality Olympics" in Chapter 5: A La Carte from Scratch. For more information on when and how the actual rules changed, refer to Chapter 6: Trends in American Dining.)

The money changers have fled from their high seats in the temple of our civilization. We may now restore that temple to the ancient truths.

—Franklin Roosevelt, 1933

****

MYTH: All politicians are corrupt.
A majority of Americans feel that they have no place in politics, that politics happens somewhere else. People see themselves as innocent victims of an ineffective political system, transferring anger at their own disempowerment into anti-government sentiment. The issue gets personalized into a mass character flaw, as if politicians were all born with sleazy DNA.

Democracy is thus, by definition, impossible, further increasing cynicism. Term limits are the logical result of this sentiment: let's remove the people without changing the system. This however, only further weakens office holders vis a vis corporate influence and entrenched bureaucracy. Amidst all this, the right positions itself as outsiders, on the side of the people.

COUNTER-STRATEGY: Show politicians as victims of corporate influence
The challenge is to shift the focus from the failed politicians to the corporations who do most of the buying. One approach is to depict politicians as spineless hirelings and eager toadies of powerful corporations. While this approach has some merits, it can backfire: deepening people's cynicism and further discrediting the democratic process.

Instead, we might try going after the system rather than the individuals. One metaphor that can help is to compare the choices confronting the politician to those facing an inner city youth. The politician can sweat it out in the district raising the necessary campaign funds from small donations or sit back and let the big easy corporate money walk right into her office. The kid in the ghetto can flip burgers or deal drugs. The trick is to portray both of these choices as systematic products of an environment that can and needs to be changed —and not as pathological character flaws.

****

MYTH: The American Dream can be "restored."
The core idea in the American Dream is that a person who works hard and plays by the rules will get ahead and be able to provide a better life for their children than the one they have. This is no longer the expectation of most Americans, largely as a result of trends towards greater economic inequality. The Republicans used the theme "restoring the American Dream" regularly at their 1996 convention, invoking a nostalgia for a simpler time with links to broader conservative cultural issues.

COUNTER-STRATEGY: Reimagine the American Dream
We can't let the Right own American Dream symbolism. First, we need to show how the American Dream was torpedoed by corporate self-interest. (To paraphrase Michael Moore, the American Dream has become "work hard, play by the rules, get fired."). And then we need to describe a new "American Dream" that is future oriented rather than nostalgic, invoking an image of a future in which everybody will share in the economic benefits.

****

MYTH: America is a classless society
In the United States discussions involving issues of class and money are often more taboo than discussing sex. Early in our lives we learn not to share the facts of our class background. As adults we avoid revealing our salary. This silence makes class invisible and supports the illusion that we live in a classless society.

COUNTER-STRATEGY: Make class visible
Confront your own internalized taboos. Find the courage to talk about class in your daily life, with friends and workmates. *How much did that cost? What are you paid? Are you making it financially?* In your more personal art, talk honestly about the role of class in your life. In your more action-oriented art, make class visible, find some way to name it—as we do with our "class choruses" in the 10 & 100 Musical Chairs (see Chapter 8: Complete Recipes).

****

MYTH: Class mobility
The American Dream is that anyone in this country can attain enough income to own his or her own home and provide comfortably for his or her family if they work hard enough. The fact that most Americans can point to at least one example where this is true reinforces the myth of class mobility and the belief that those who don't move up lack a strong work ethic.

COUNTER-STRATEGY: Show systematic barriers to equal opportunity
While it is true that there is some class fluidity in the U.S. and that class status may change over the lifetimes of many individuals, the reality is that class

It is a cruel jest to say to a bootless man that he should lift himself by his own bootstraps. It is even worse to tell a man to lift himself by his own bootstraps when somebody is standing on the boot.

—Martin Luther King, Jr.

is much less fluid than most people think.

One study showed that one's father's occupation is the best predictor of one's potential income level—more important than IQ, level of education, or years in the work force.

Think what you believe.
photo Ellen Shub

A study United for a Fair Economy did of the Forbes 400—the 400 richest people in America—showed that behind all the Horatio Alger mythology, most of the very wealthy inherited their wealth. Over the last 15 years government policies have rewarded asset holders at the expense of income earners, making it more difficult than ever for the rest of us to move up the economic ladder.

****

MYTH: History is the progress of dead rich white men
History is usually taught from the perspective of the privileged. Much of what we learn in school, for example, is told from the perspective of political and military leaders who are usually members of the upper classes. The perceptions and realities of everyday working people are rarely explored.

The most common and durable source of faction has been the various and unequal distribution of property...Our Republic will be an impossibility because wealth will be in the hands of a few.

—James Madison, The Federalist No. 10

COUNTER-STRATEGY: Tell the other half of the story
With a few witty words the popular bumper sticker, "The labor movement: the people who brought you the weekend" shows us just how central the labor movement has been in the history of our country.

We need to celebrate labor's story. We need to tell the story of the resistance to classism and the history of the mass movements that have risen up to redistribute wealth and reduce inequality in our country, from the populist Agrarian movement in the 1890's to the union movement and Share Our Wealth Societies of the 1930's.

****

MYTH: Economics is for experts
Economic concepts often feel overwhelming for folks who are unfamiliar with even the basics (e.g. the difference between gross and net income, GNP, profit, the difference between salary and wages, or the difference between income and wealth). Math anxiety and math phobia contribute to a feeling of disempowerment or distrust of statistical information.

COUNTER-STRATEGY: Make economics "popular"
Use familiar metaphors. Make it interactive, physical and fun. Set aside the details for later. Make it connect directly to people's lives. Boil down the numbers to simple ratios and proportions. Tell it like a story of "what's going on."

****

MYTH: Democracy and Capitalism are one and the same
MYTH: Pointing out inequality is class warfare, rich bashing, and jealous envy
MYTH: A critique of the economic order is an attack on democracy
During the Cold War between the U.S. and the Soviet Union, capitalism

and communism became polarized. Capitalism was equated with democracy and communism was equated with undemocratic and totalitarian political systems.

To many people, challenging the US economic system means challenging democracy. When you raise issues of class inequality, you get labeled "anti-democratic," an advocate of "class warfare," "communist," "red," or "unpatriotic," with the effect of marginalizing or silencing criticism of the economic structure.

This "red-baiting" prevents any careful examination of U.S. economic policies or consideration of alternative economic policies and structures within a democratic framework.

COUNTER-STRATEGY: Democracy and fairness are one and the same
A fair economy with equal opportunity for all is essential to the functioning of a real democracy. Growing income and wealth inequality have put too much power in the hands of corporations and the very wealthy. Just witness how our electoral process has been hijacked by big money interests and corporate donors.

With the rich controlling our democratic institutions, the rules governing our economy have been tilted to benefit large asset owners at the expense of people who work for a living. Demanding greater fairness and equality is completely consistent with our national ideals and traditions. In fact, it is necessary if we are to preserve democracy.

☆☆☆☆☆☆☆☆☆

MYTH: It's all hopeless and we're helpless
The intensity of feelings of hopelessness and helplessness that arise when we focus on the vastness of inequality can be overwhelming. Many strategies just seem too insignificant in comparison to the immensity of the problem.

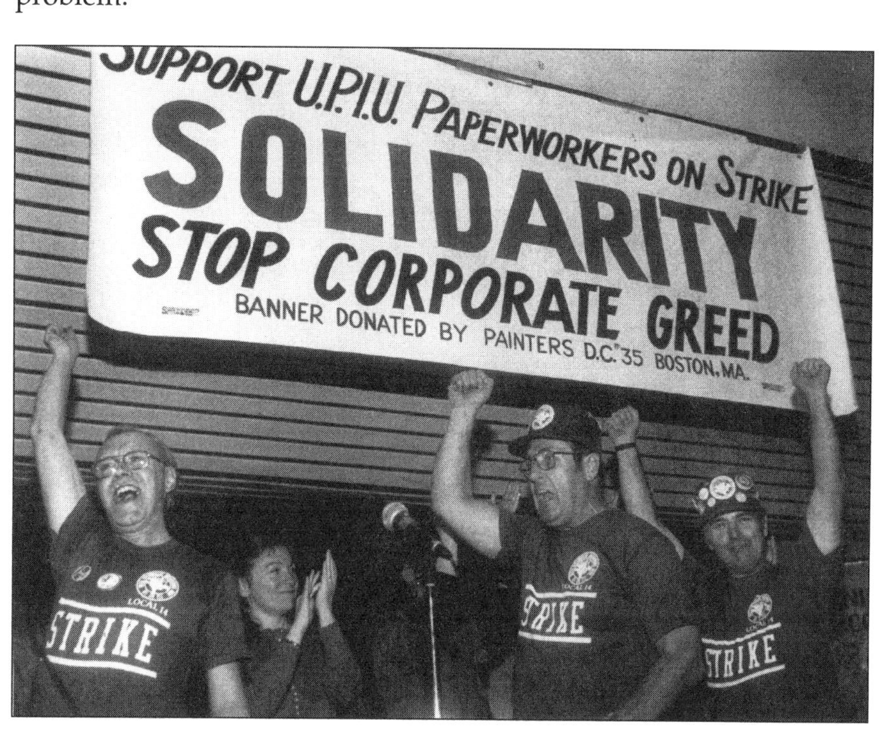

Strike! Support rally for striking paper workers from the International Paper plant in Jay, Maine, 1989.
photo Ellen Shub

COUNTER-STRATEGY: History shows that we can change the system
Every time in our history when wealth has become as concentrated as it is today, a mass movement has risen up to correct the injustice. In the 1880's and 1930's, when inequality was very extreme, people came together to work for fairness. In the 1950's and 1960's strong unions, government policies like the GI Bill and the Home Mortgage Program, and a social commitment to equal opportunity resulted in greater levels of equality. The rules were changed in the 70's and 80's. Although this benefited the wealthy, it shows us that it is within our grasp to change things—this time to again benefit the majority.

In 1996 Tony Roma, founder of the rib restaurant chain of the same name, was actively lobbying against a living wage campaign in Oregon. Just before lunch rush at the Portland franchise, Jobs with Justice supporters trickled in by two's and three's until, unknown to management, they had filled many of the seats in the restaurant.

At this point a 6 foot 2 organizer from the letter carrier's union, sauntered in, dressed as Marie Antoinette, in full costume, with an 18th century style powdered wig and a couple of attendants in waiting.

He walked right past the shocked managers to the center of the restaurant and addressed the hushed customers: "Tony Roma is saying, 'let them eat cake.' So let's have some cake." And then he and his attendants proceeded to give out slices of cake to everyone in the restaurant. Supporters then started chanting, "Lousy sauce! Lousy boss! Don't eat here!" Oregon now has the highest minimum wage in the country.

If you are looking for action-performances that are already worked out and battle tested, you've come to the right place. The four recipes included in this chapter were home cooked here in Boston by Art for a Fair Economy and allied organizations. Over the last year and half, we have performed them throughout the US and in Canada. Here you will find everything you need to put them on. Just add energy, passion, and a twist of your own imagination, to taste.

Each recipe includes a short description, ingredient list, preparation and serving instructions, full script, stage layout diagrams and additional statistical information as needed.

IMPORTANT NOTE: The 10 Musical Chairs and 100 Musical Chairs have much in common: they share the same script, use many of the same props, etc. But because they also differ in important ways, we chose to describe each in a separate and complete recipe. In this way, you get all the information you need in one place, whichever of these performances you decide to do.

Description
The Rich People's Liberation Front*—the "radical fringe" of the US's wealthiest 1%—is a fictitious entity that can be used in many creative ways, including: guerrilla theater, media hoax, satirical event, or heckling that plays off a straight event. In the last year, members of the RPLF (and a sister group, the "Fat Cats"), costumed in tuxedos, cigars and furs, have been seen all over New England, dissing the poor at their own "Rally for the Rich," glad-handing taxpayers outside the post office, and toasting their favorite corporate-friendly politician on the steps of the State Capitol.

Ingredients

2 or more performers

top hats, tuxedos, business suits, "power" ties, big plastic cigars, cellular phones

evening gowns, gaudy jewelry, mink stoles, fur coats

pillows or other padding to bulk up the characters

wads of fake money pouring out of every pocket

furry ears and tail, and eye liner for whiskers et al (for the "Fat Cats" variant)

stretch limo: "the only way to travel"

Versions
Guerrilla Leafleting. On tax day glad-hand the lines of taxpayers outside post offices, thanking them for their contributions and continuing cooperation. On election days, work busy polling places, with the line "a vote for [X candidate] is a vote for the really rich." Put on a short skit or monologue rant to attract additional attention.

Show of Unwanted Support. Choose an appropriate target and occasion (appearance by candidate or elected official, annual board of directors meeting, fundraising dinner, legislative vote...etc.) and make a big show of enthusiastic support. The idea here is to embarrass the target and link him in people's minds to the very wealthy.

Here in Massachusetts, we've staged a "Rally for the Really Rich", had a champagne toast on the steps of the State House, declared a "Tax Loophole Protection Day" and given out "Silver Spoon Awards."

To create an especially attractive photo-op, one member of your group might try to physically reach the target, shake his hand and express support in a quick double-edged one-

liner. As part of any of these actions, hold a press conference and give out leaflets.

Heckling. Provide comical counterpoint to a straight movement event. Get invited to heckle a press conference. Hold a mock hostile counterdemonstration, complete with slogans painted on signs, chants and handouts.

Use heckling judiciously, not to disrupt the main event but to complement it and give it comic relief. Always try to work hand-in-hand with the organizers of the straight event. You might plan for the MC of the straight event to indulge your concerns and magnanimously invite one of your group up to the mike to speak. Always stay in character.

Remember, the idea here is to add spice and curiosity to a straight event or demonstration, strengthening its message by painting a fully absurd picture in the opposite direction.

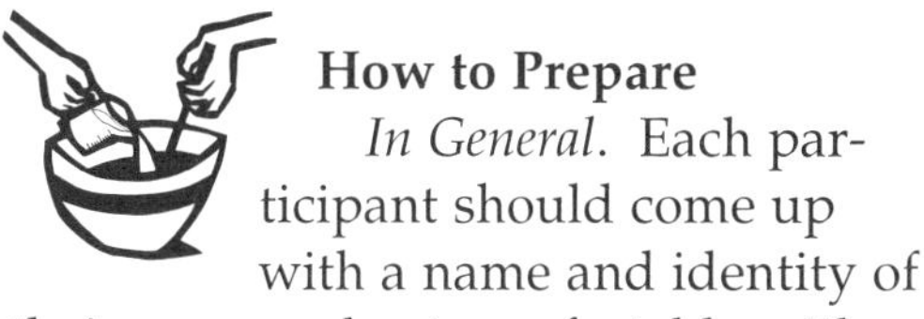

How to Prepare

In General. Each participant should come up with a name and identity of their own, and get comfortable with a few good lines.

How to Serve

In General. Stay in character through out each event. Where necessary, assign a support person to handle out-of-character tasks or to respond seriously to questions from your audience and the media. Or take a cue from the Fat Cats who use a character called "Radical Rat" to speak the truth.

Leaflets. Create a leaflet that has your serious message on one side and a computer modified image of a large bill on the other. People respond to the image of money.

Spice to Taste

Limousine. Arrive at any of these events by limousine.

Variations. You could try other variations on this theme including: "People for the Protection of the Really Rich" or "The CEO's Charity Fund" or the Michael Moore inspired, "Corp-Aid."

Media Hoax. Consider going all the way with your fictitious identity and really trying to hoax the media into believing you are for real. Tone it down: make it seem feasible yet still bizarre. Set up an answering machine with a professional sounding message. Use your own stationary. If the media bites, ride it as far as you can. Then hold a press conference unveiling the hoax.

*The Rich People's Liberation Front is a wholly-owned subsidiary of the Massachusetts Human Services Coalition. The character of Thurston Morton Beechcraft Collingsworth IV is the alter-ego of the Coalition's Vice President, Steve Collins. While they are happy to share the concept, please credit them if either is used.

Chants
The rich, united, have never been defeated!

Take to your car phones, take to your faxes,
Join the fight to end all taxes!

To hell with the needy, take care of the greedy!

Who needs day care, hire an au pair!

Songs
This land is my land, this land is my land, this land is my land...

One-liners
Thank you for paying more than your fair share (of taxes).

All of our tax cuts over the last fifteen years wouldn't have been possible without your faithful cooperation.

We simply didn't have time to write thank you notes to everyone.

How can the rich get richer if the poor won't get poorer?

We deserve the best politicians our money can buy.

We are a buy-partisan group...we buy Republicans and we buy Democrats.

We're paying for America's free elections (so you won't have to).

Bribery will get you everything.

Character Names
Phil T. Rich
Bill Fold
Cashman E. Leet
Dolly Bill
Aphelia Doe
U. R. Conned
Dewey, Cheatum & Howe

Sample Identity
Thurston Morton Beechcraft Collingsworth IV

CEO of Incorporated, Inc.

Mr. Collingsworth earned his wealth the old fashioned way—he inherited it and has watched it multiply since his birth and upbringing on the family's estate in Manchester-by-the-Sea, where he still enjoys the Good Life with his lovely spouse, Priscilla Elizabeth Farnsworth (nee Chadwicke) Collingsworth and assorted children, thorough-bred horses, hunting dogs and servants.

In 1985, in Corvallis Oregon, the Forest Service had reserved an auditorium for a huge Smokey the Bear birthday party for elementary school children. Earth First! decided to crash the party. They printed a leaflet (in big letters so a child could read it) saying that it was 10 times more likely that Smokey's favorite forest would be destroyed by logging than by a forest fire.

Grizzly being read his rights. Earth First! Yellowstone Park action, July, 1985. *photo David Cross*

One Earth First! member dressed up in a Smokey the Bear costume (the Forest Service's own Smokey the Bear costume had been destroyed in the wash) and walked into the party. He was immediately surrounded by a sea of adoring kids and started giving out flyers.

The rangers tried to forcibly eject Smokey from the premises without letting on to the kids that anything was wrong, eventually knocking his costume head off. The next day it was logging, not careless use of matches, that dominated the front page of the paper.

Description

The Rat Race humorously portrays the unequal income growth that has occurred among different economic levels over the last fifteen years. It is a sporting-event spoof with play-by-play TV announcers, cheerleaders et al. Different runners in the "rat race" represent different economic strata, and the number of steps they take forward (or backward) during the race accurately represents the growth (or loss) of income during the recent period. The results of the race paint a brutal picture of economic disparity which the skit cuts with humor.

The Rat Race can be performed outdoors as street theater or indoors as a staged skit, on its own or as one of a series of similar skits in an "Inequality Olympics" type format. It comes in gourmet, homestyle and microwave versions. (Those of you who have participated in United for a Fair Economy's popular education workshop, will recognize this skit as a dramatization of our "Growing Together, Growing Apart" role play.)

How to Prepare

Memorization. This piece works best if performers can commit their lines to memory. Most of the lines are the announcer's, so with one or two very committed people memorization should not be too difficult.

Cheerleaders. The cheerleaders really add something. Both men and women can play this role. The cheerleaders should try to be earnest, enthusiastic and as much like real cheerleaders as possible (if they do this, the chants themselves will provide the comic tension). They should avoid making fun of the cheerleader form itself or backing off of a full-throated embrace of the role. Try to find actual matching cheerleader outfits. Otherwise, try to find pleated skirts and turtleneck shirts in two matching colors. For additional effect, you may wish to add dollar signs or rat outlines to the shirts with fabric paint.

Number of steps. Each step a runner takes forward (or backward) represents a 5% change in income. Thus the exact number of steps each runner takes is a very important detail and should be given the proper attention in rehearsal and performance. (See stage diagram.)

Salary numbers. An equally important, though technically tricky, part of the performance are the runner's salary numbers. These show the actual beginning and ending income statistics for each runner and should be used, if possible. Securely attach the end-

INGREDIENTS -- RAT RACE

	gourmet 	homestyle 	microwave 
space:	60 ft 10 ft	60 ft x 10 ft	60 ft x 10 ft
performance time:	10 minutes	7 minutes	5 minutes
set up time:	5 minutes	5 minutes	5 minutes
prep time:	2-3 rehearsals	1-2 rehearsals	1 rehearsal
performers:			
heavily involved	2	2	1
modestly involved	6	6	3
lightly involved	6	2	
props:	script	script	script
	2 suits	2 suits	1 suit
	2 name cards	2 name cards	
	7 rat noses	3 rat noses	3 rat noses
	7 sweat pants	3 sweat pants	
	7 running shoes	3 running shoes	
	7 shirts & ties	3 shirts & ties	
	7 race number sets	3 race number sets	3 race number sets
	safety pins	safety pins	safety pins
	Velcro strips	Velcro strips	
	1 referee outfit	1 referee outfit	
	3 cheerleader outfits	3 cheerleader outfits	
	1 flip chart & easel		
Notes on versions	The version described throughout this recipe entry.	Drop the 4 runners that have no spoken lines (keeping the 3 runners with spoken lines: Bottom 20%, Middle 20%, and Top 1%). Cut down the script. Also, if necessary, drop the referee and the cheerleaders.	Drop all items dropped by the "Homestyle" version. Plus, as necessary, drop the music, merge the two commentators, and further cut down the announcer's lines as you see fit. Also, you can drop the runners' salary numbers from the performance or simplify their preparation and use by having each runner hold and show them by hand instead of attaching them to their shirts. Alternately, each runner could wear their beginning salary number but have the announcer present them with their ending salary number at the end of the race.

ing number to the runner's shirt with the Velcro or safety pins. Then attach the beginning number on top of the ending number but *only* secure it at its *top* edge so it acts like a hinge that can be flipped up at the end of the race to reveal the ending salary number underneath. In addition, attach Velcro to the shirt and number so that after it is flipped up, it can be pinned back. (See point in script where announcer indicates changes in the runners' salaries.)

How to Serve

Indoors. Might try performing skit in an aisle, if wide enough.

Outdoors. Requires a long strip of space to perform, thus not appropriate for a street corner or "in the round." Need to clear out that space ahead of time and gather audience alongside it. In this way, audience gets the most dramatic cross-section view of the different distances the runners travel. Sidewalk too narrow to both perform and gather an audience.

Music. Music is also a great help to this performance—either live or via boom box. Trumpet fanfare is an excellent way to announce the beginning of the piece and a rendition (or actual cut) of the "Chariots of Fire" theme song by Vangelis works perfectly during the race itself .

Spice to Taste

Develop the cheerleaders further. Create lots of your own chants, develop synchronized movements for each chant (maybe working in some gymnastic moves), add more cheerleaders, choose to make it a completely cross-dressed squad, elaborate the costumes.

Add to the set. Add a finish line tape (10 steps after start line). Lay down track lanes, calibrated in increments of each 10% change in income.

Develop the text of the TV announcers. Add a WIOU jingle. Add a spoof advertisement. Add local flavor to the runners' characters and personal stories.

Involve the audience. Near the end of the skit, when announcer is saying "many fans are saying that the race is rigged...", have the announcer actually go up to individual audience members and interview them, polling their feelings on the topic. To do this well, announcer must stay in character and keep things moving.

Middle Man runs furiously just to stay in place.
Meg Stone, with nose, runs the *Rat Race* at the 100th anniversary of the Boston Marathon, April, 1996.
photo Mike Massey

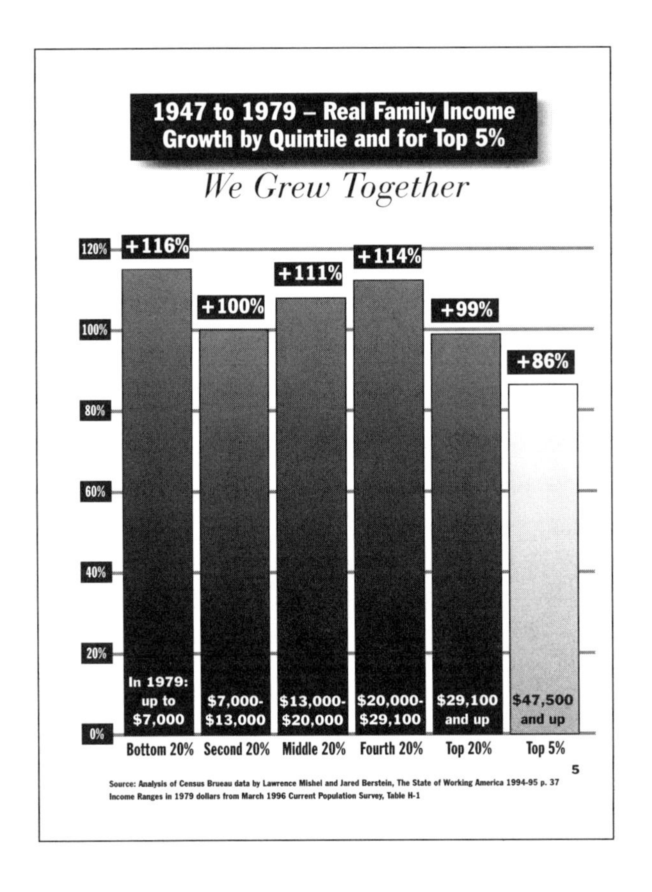

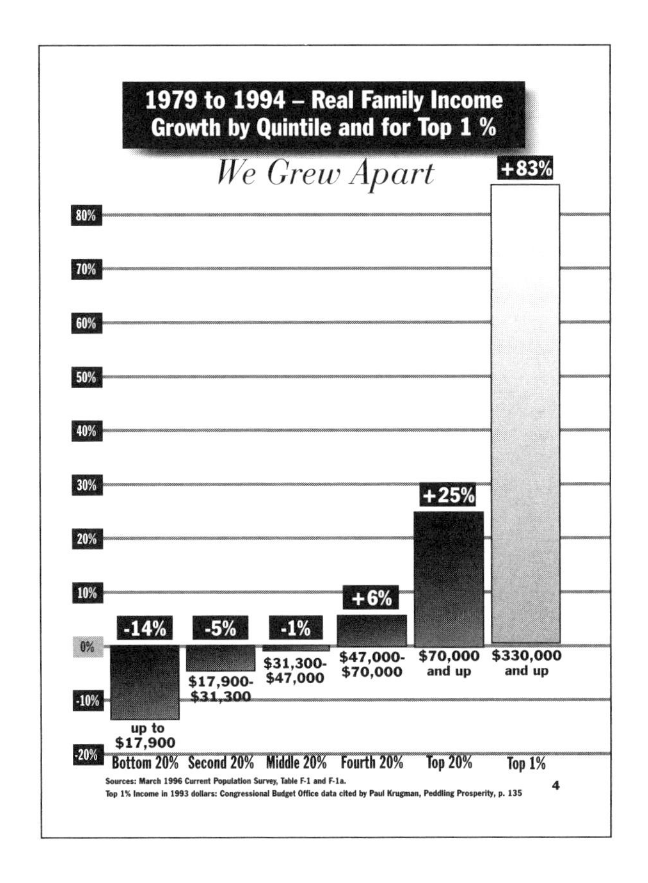

RUNNER INFO:

(Best available data at time of original performance.)

Strata	Name	1979 Income**	Strides* (% Change)	1993 Income**
Bottom 20	Bottom Dollar	$9,000	-4 (-20%)	$7,000
Second 20		$18,000	-2 (-10%)	$16,000
Middle 20	Middle Man	$26,000	-1 (-5%)	$25,000
Fourth 20		$33,000	+1 (+5%)	$35,000
Top 20		$70,000	+3 (+15%)	$80,000
Top 5		$120,000	+5 (+25%)	$150,000
Top 1	Top Dog	$190,000	+22 (+110%)	$400,000

* Negative numbers indicate backward strides. Positive numbers indicate forward strides.

** All dollars are in constant 1979 dollars.

Originally performed at the 100th anniversary of the Boston Marathon
April 15, 1996.

Scene 1:	Pre-Race Warm-Up
Scene 2:	Race
Scene 3:	Post-Race Wrap Up
Extra:	Cheerleader Cheers

Shorthand	Character	Costume
MC	Emcee/Announcer	suit, mike
CC	Color Commentator	suit, ear piece, mike
B20	Bottom 20% ("Bottom Dollar")	shirt & tie above waist,
S20	Second 20%	running gear below waist,
M20	Middle 20% ("Middle Man")	rat noses,
F20	Fourth 20%	race #'s front & back
T20	Top 20%	as above
T5	Top 5%	as above
T1	Top 1% ("Top Dog")	as above, plus bowler hat
REF	Referee	black and white stripes
CL1	Cheerleader 1	matching outfits:
CL2	Cheerleader 2	pleated skirt and
CL3	Cheerleader 3	turtle neck decorated w/ "$" signs
MU	Music/Trumpeteer	cool jazz look

Scene 1: PRE-RACE WARM-UP

(Cheerleaders do their pre-game set of cheers, attracting onlookers...)

(Runners are warming up, running in place, stretching...etc.)

MC: Welcome back to WIOU's Widening World of Sports. I'm here with Bob-Cost-Us-A-Lot. We now pause in our coverage of the 100th anniversary of the Boston Marathon...and turn our attention to the race all of us are running, yes, the one we run every day of our lives: the rat race.

MC: As with all rat races, the runners here today are competing for income. They have come from every corner of the economy, from the bottom 20% to the top 1%, to compete here today. The runners will begin in their 1979 positions. Each stride they advance represents a 5% growth in income. How far will they get? We'll see in just a few minutes...

MC: So, Bob, what can past races tell us about the results we might see today......

CC: Not very much, Dave, not much. You see, Dave, it's just not the same sport it used to be. (Flips up chart of income growth 1950-1978.) Looking here, you can see the results from the last time these athletes all competed against each other. The period was 1950 to 1978, and as you can see it was a pretty even contest. Income for all of the competitors rose steadily. But you know, Dave, most commentators feel the sport has changed a lot since then. No one knows what to expect today.

MC: Thanks, Bob. And now tell us...who should we be looking out for today?

CC: First up, in lane 7, from Dorchester, Mass, we have Bottom Dollar (runner raises hands). Carrying the banner for the bottom 20% of the population today, the hopes and dreams of new immigrants, fast food workers and the underemployed are all riding on her economic performance today.

CC: And at the other end of the track, in lane 1, from Beacon Hill, we have the venerable, Top Dog, running for the richest 1% of the population today. He's the favorite of top surgeons, overpaid media stars and the idle rich everywhere. In the last few years, he's become a truly multi-national powerhouse.

CC: And finally, rounding out the field in lane 5, from Quincy, Mass., our very own Middle Man, representing the middle 20% of the population. Once the defining presence of the sport, this tough competitor has been hamstrung by a series of injuries, forcing her to run tag-team with the spouse on the off-season. And that's about it, Dave, back to you.

MC: Thanks, Bob. All of these athletes have incredible stories. We'll just have to see how these various factors play themselves out...

MC: And looking over at the referee, it seems we're about to get under way... the runners are now taking their 1979 starting positions... and, remember fans: each stride forward is a 5% growth in income...

Scene 2: THE RACE

REF: On your marks. Get set. Go! (Fires cap gun or blows whistle.)

MC: And they're off!

(Scene goes into another space: a more inward, dramatic, slow-motion pace.)

(Runners move simultaneously in exaggerated slow motion.)

(Runners move forward or backward according to the table at end of script:)

(Bottom Dollar moves as if running into an incredibly strong head wind, for a brief moment leaning over the starting line but then being blown backwards 4 strides.)

(Middle Man runs in place very rapidly and then at the very end, puts her two feet together and takes a half-step jump backwards.)

(Top Dog moves forward 22 steps in long, loping, caricatured, high-stepping strides.)

(All runners stay in their final positions until skit is over.)

(During race, EITHER:

1) Musician plays theme from Chariots of Fire

OR

2) MC & CC keep up an improvised, very rapid, run-together, play-by-play commentary, based on the following:)

MC/CC: In lane 1, we've got...trickle down, real-estate speculation, initial public offerings...
In lane 5, we've got downsizing, permanent displacement, and no benefits...
In lane 7, we've got plant shutdowns, low-wages, temp work, and run away shops,
Labor unions are under attack...
Big money is gaining control of politics...
Tax cuts seem to be favoring the wealthy....
Government services are being cut across the board...
The salaries of top corporate executives are quadrupling...
National debt seems to be tripling...
Health care costs are exploding...
Minimum wage is falling behind inflation...

MC: And it's all over folks. That's it. The race is run. And we've got clear winners and losers today. A staggering triumph for privilege. A crushing defeat for the less fortunate. The fans are stunned.

Scene 3: POST-RACE RAP UP

MC: We go now to the field, to get some perspective on this truly polarizing outcome ...

MC: ...Bottom Dollar, running today for the bottom 20%, you experienced a truly punishing loss, down to an income of $7,000 [rips off 1979 salary to reveal 1993 salary]...what happened out there...?

B20: I was working hard out there Dave, I was struggling the whole time, but it was brutal. Right from the start, I just seemed to be slipping further and further behind...there wasn't even a safety net to catch me...

MC: ...Bottom Dollar, what is going through your head right at this very moment?

B20: In part I blame myself, Dave, but it also makes me ANGRY... it's just not the same sport anymore, Dave. Making minimum wage, with no health care, I just can't keep up. Some of us rats just don't have a chance anymore...

MC: It's been a tough couple of decades for you Bottom Dollar, but I'm sure the fans are hurting right along with you. Maybe you need to pick up another job or two between seasons. Well, hang tough and good luck to you...

MC: ... and Middle Man, representing the middle 20%, you were stagnating out there today, dropping back to $25,000 [rips off 1979 salary to reveal 1993 salary]...how do you feel...?

M20: frankly, Dave, I'm still stunned... [pant]... I was running hard, really hard, but I just couldn't seem to make any headway at all. With wave after wave of corporate downsizing, I never feel secure. I just don't see how I'll ever get to buy a house, or put my kids through college, even if I retrain all season...

MC: I'm sure a lot of fans share your concerns today, Middle Man. With so many middle-class hopes and American dreams pinned on Middle Man's performance, it's surely a dark day for the American rat race...

MC: But even though more than 60% of the population didn't make it out of the starting gate today, it's not all bad news... on the bright side, and the surprise of the afternoon, and racking up a triumph unprecedented in the history of the sport, we have Top Dog. Running today for the richest 1%, you swept the field, more than doubling your income to $400,000 [rips off 1979 salary to reveal 1993 salary]. Congratulations!

T1: [compared to the other runners, an air of victory and proud calm]
Thanks, Dave, thanks. Yeah, I have to say, it's a really sweet victory, sweeter than I ever expected. The conditions were all in my favor; I just went out there and did my privileged best. But you know, Dave, I never could have done it alone; I had the whole team behind me. I want to take this opportunity to thank my lobbyists and government inside players. They made it possible for me to cut my taxes, ship jobs overseas, and bust unions. Together we've put in a lot of hard years and today it just paid off!

Scene 3: POST-RACE WRAP UP (Continued...)

MC: Congratulations, Top Dog, and the fans seem to think you earned every million of it! Your victory today surely marks the transition to a whole new economy...Where to now?

T1: I'm going to Disney World!! (And maybe I'll buy it!)

MC: Well, we've just heard from the runners and clearly today's results dramatically confirm something we've been hearing a lot about lately: the vast and growing divide between the very, very richest rats and the rest of us. In fact, all this year we've heard grumblings from the fans that the race is rigged. Bob, how true is this? and what's being done?

CC: Well, Dave, down here in the field I can tell you it's true all right: a lot of fans are telling us that the race isn't fair. They're saying that to bring this sport back to respectability, we need a major policy overhaul. We need a radical change in the rules of the game in order to level the playing field. And these fans already have a lot of ideas about what kinds of changes we need. We've heard calls for an end to corporate welfare, an increase in the minimum wage and electoral reform to get big money out of politics.

MC: Thanks, Bob. Clearly there is a strong sentiment for change out there. But the big question, Dave, is whether those fans who want change will talk it up, organize and press home their demands. It's really up to them. The future of the sport is in their hands.

MC: And that's it for today. Thank you for tuning into WIOU's Widening World of Sports. We now return you to live coverage of the Boston Marathon.

CHEERLEADER CHEERS

2, 4, 6, 8, how do stocks appreciate
Wall Street, Wall Street, Yeaaaaa!!! Wall Street!

Corporate power, corporate power!
Send the losers to the shower!

Helmsley, Milken, Boesky, Trump!
We've got money up our rump!

The wealthy, the wealthy, we gotta keep 'em healthy!
The poor, the poor, kick 'em out the door!

Donald Trump, he's our man!
If he can't do it, no one can!

Description

10 Musical Chairs is a participatory performance that dramatizes the growing disparity between the very rich and everyone else. 10 chairs (each representing 10% of the US wealth) are arranged in a line. 10 participants (each representing 10% of the US population) sit on the chairs in a series of "human bar graphs" that portray with statistical accuracy the increasingly unequal distribution of US wealth. (In the final 1997 arrangement, the person representing the richest 10% spreads himself out across 7 chairs while the remaining 9 people pile on top of each other in the remaining 3 chairs.)

During the performance, participants (both those in the chairs and in the larger audience) are led by a conductor, dressed in full tuxedo and tails, through a five-movement chanted choral performance, complete with soloists, and sections representing the working, middle and upper classes.

10 Musical Chairs can be performed indoors at union conventions, activist conferences, and school assemblies as well as outdoors at festivals, or rallies. (Those of you who have participated in United for a Fair Economy's popular education workshops, will recognize the 10 Musical Chairs as dramatizations of our 10 Chairs role play.)

How to Prepare

10 Chairs or 100 Chairs? If you're not sure whether the 10 Musical Chairs or the 100 Musical Chairs (see next recipe) is more appropriate for your needs, consider the following summary of their similarities and differences. They apply the same concept and use virtually the same script. The 100 Musical Chairs is 10 times bigger, quite a bit more spectacular, involves more people in a more physical way, shows a higher level of statistical detail, but requires a lot more room and is a lot more complicated to set up, perform and break down.

In general, the 10 Musical Chairs gives you more for your dollar. We also recommend it for all indoor settings other than school gymnasiums or the like. The 100 Musical Chairs is best done outside, on a college green, for example, and in settings where the media attention you can leverage from the sheer extraordinary size and spectacle of it makes it worth the extra effort.

Choosing a venue. Because the text of the piece is important, your venue must carry sound well. Because participation is the backbone of the piece, the larger the audience, the better. Because the piece tells a story and the audience is instructed early on how to participate, it is best to have an audience that will stay with you from beginning to end. Because when the piece works well, it can get very loud, choose a venue where this is not a problem.

INGREDIENTS -- 10 MUSICAL CHAIRS

	gourmet	**homestyle**	**microwave** 
space:	20 ft x 10 ft	20 ft x 10 ft	20 ft x 10 ft
performance time:	15-20 minutes	15-20 minutes	15 minutes
set up time:	5 minutes	2-3 minutes	1 minute
prep time:	5 hours*	3 hours*	1/2 hour*
performers:			
heavily involved	1	1	1
modestly involved	5	3	
lightly involved	5	7	10
props:	1 conductor's tux	1 conductor's tux	1 black suit
	appropriate clothing		
	10 chairs	10 chairs	10 chairs
	90+ feather dusters	9 feather dusters	
	10+ bowler hats	1 bowler hat	1 black hat or shades
Notes on versions	Use a full 5 soloists, one for each part in the script. Rehearse well, particularly the solos in movement 4 and the call and response in movement 5. Have soloists wear clothing appropriate to their social class. Give out lots of extra feather dusters and bowler hats to the audience just prior to the performance.	Piece can be handily done with just 3 soloists. Have the middle class soloist play both middle class solo parts. Likewise, have the working class soloist play both working class solo parts. Have bowler hats and feather dusters for the performers but not the audience.	Can be performed in a quick and dirty fashion. Drop movement 4. Instead of memorizing lines, participants can read from the scripts during the performance. If really pressed for time, at a busy conference, for example, soloists can be found as little as 1/2 hour before the performance and pressed into service. Also, the piece can be performed effectively with minimal or no props: Use a black suit of some kind in place of the conductor's tux. Any kind of hat or dark sunglasses will work for the richest 10%. Perform without any feather dusters.

*Does not include Conductor's prep time.

Obtaining props. Feather dusters can be purchased at Woolworth's, departments stores, local hardware stores, etc. for approximately $1.50/per. However, it is unlikely you will find more than 20, never mind 90+, in any one place. Stores will order them in bulk if you arrange it. Give enough time for delivery and work out a wholesale discount. Also, buy one extra that is especially elegant, the conductor can use it as a baton.

BEGIN

Bowler hats can be purchased at local costume or joke shops. The low-end versions go for about $7/per. A conductor's tux can be rented from any tux shop for about $65. Also, in any major city, there should be at least one store that sells used tuxes where you might be able to pick up a full outfit for about $125. If you are doing performances on two or more separate days, it might pay to buy.

1976

Chairs. Any chairs will do but the chairs that work best are sturdy, narrow, easy to move, and have no arms. Some institutional-style chairs snap together and this can help increase stability. Some people prefer that all the chairs be the same shape and color (often, black). Others find it interesting to have an odd assortment of chairs. In either case, **you must have exactly 10 chairs**—no more and no less.

1997

Setting up the chairs. Line up 10 chairs alongside each other facing the audience, either in a straight line or a gentle arc. It helps to place the widest and sturdiest of your chairs in the rightmost locations, as these will have to bear the greatest load.

How to Serve

The Conductor. The conductor is the linchpin of the 10 Musical Chairs. If he (or she) is well prepared and practiced, then the piece will work, no matter how well everything else comes together. His secret is that, while disguised as a formal conductor, he is elegantly directing, stage managing and MCing the whole show right as it happens. He is able to begin, end and modulate all the choruses, orchestrate a raw audience, and cue ill-prepared soloists—all from within the show, without anyone noticing or caring. This is why the microwave version can work so well with so little other preparation.

Which chairs to sit on. As the piece proceeds, the performers must change their seating arrangements to reflect changing patterns of wealth distribution. Use the graphics on this page as a guide. In addition, the performance breaks the group of 9 into a middle class chorus of 4 and a working class chorus of 5. These choruses should try to stay clustered together, with the working class closer to the end chair. Before the piece begins, make sure all performers know what class they are supposed to be in and what chairs they should be sitting in at the various stages.

How to "sit" on the chairs. For most of the performance, 9 people have to find a way to sit on 3 chairs. Some people feel uncomfortable sitting in a stranger's lap, while for others it's a hoot. Others, such as elderly, disabled, or very large people, may have more physical concerns. Be sensitive to these differences. Use rehearsals to help performers get comfortable and experiment.

This is a "human sculpture." It's as much art as any other part of the performance. Have fun and make it interesting. Find arrangements that straddle more than one chair. Use different height levels. Try sitting on the back of a chair or standing on the seat. Try to convey tension. What you <u>don't</u> want is a really static set up like one person sitting on a chair, another on the floor in front of it and a third standing behind it. One rule of thumb that sometimes works is that everyone must be on a chair in some way.

Giving out props to the audience. Just prior to the show have a few volunteers selectively hand out bowler hats to the section of the audience most to the actors' right and to the audience's left. Generously distribute feather dusters to everyone else. When done correctly, the upper class section of the audience should mirror the upper class section of the performers sitting in the 10 chairs, and so on for the other classes.

Tips and Tricks for the Conductor. You should play the Conductor big and with a lot of authority. Use physical humor. Play off the audience and improvise. During the choruses, some one will often trail off after everyone else has cut off. You can get a lot of laughs out of these moments, by shooting them a look or making an off-hand comment.

Come up with your own one-liners. You might encourage the Middle Class to get louder with their "Get a job!" chant, by saying, "Come on Middle Class, this is <u>your</u> mantra!" Or you might encourage the Working class to use their feather dusters, by saying, "Wave those feather dusters! Whaddya think they are? The hammer and sickle of the service economy?!" Think about your entrance. Be dramatic but clear with your conducting signals. Use the video as a guide.

Rehearsing the audience. At the appropriate time in the performance (see attached script), the conductor will identify sections of the audience by class and instruct them on how to join in on the choruses, etc. The rehearsal can actually be one of the richest and most fun moments in the piece because it foreshadows the whole performance and it is the moment when the audience is first really getting into the act. It is the key moment for

establishing a good bond with the audience.

Performing at a rally or demonstration. The 10 chairs provides a great format for part of a rally program: the conductor fills the role of inspirational speaker, the performance chants fill the role of chanted slogans and yet the whole thing is refreshingly different. There are a few additional things to consider: get the ten performers and their chairs high enough so everyone can see them, plan out ahead of time how you are going to crisply pass the microphone back and forth among conductor and soloists, take special care to get the feather dusters and/or bowler hats back from the audience, if you pass them out.

Spice to Taste

Encourage the performers to improvise. The Upper Class Soloist might embellish his lines with ranting and raving or add more complexity to his character by showing some doubt or anxiety or guilt. The middle and working class soloists might adapt their lines to better reflect the images and language of their own lives.

Backdrop. Paint a banner with a slogan or a mural-like visual story and place it behind the 10 chairs for the performance.

Customize the script. Write a new movement, complete with its own chorus lines and solos, that addresses the particular issues and concerns of your audience. Add it in to the middle or use it in place of an existing movement (movement 4 is a good one to replace).

Additional Resources Available

Video. A video of the 10 Chairs is available from United for a Fair Economy. The video can help in a multitude of ways: generating interest, hearing the exact rhythms of the chants, seeing how to arrange things spatially, etc. It is highly recommended. ($10)

Translation. A full Spanish translation of the script and a partial Haitian Creole translation are also available. (free)

Complete Action Kit. Everything you need to do the gourmet version of the 10 Chairs (except the tuxedo), including: video, 10 bowler hats, 100 feather dusters, etc. (inquire as to price)

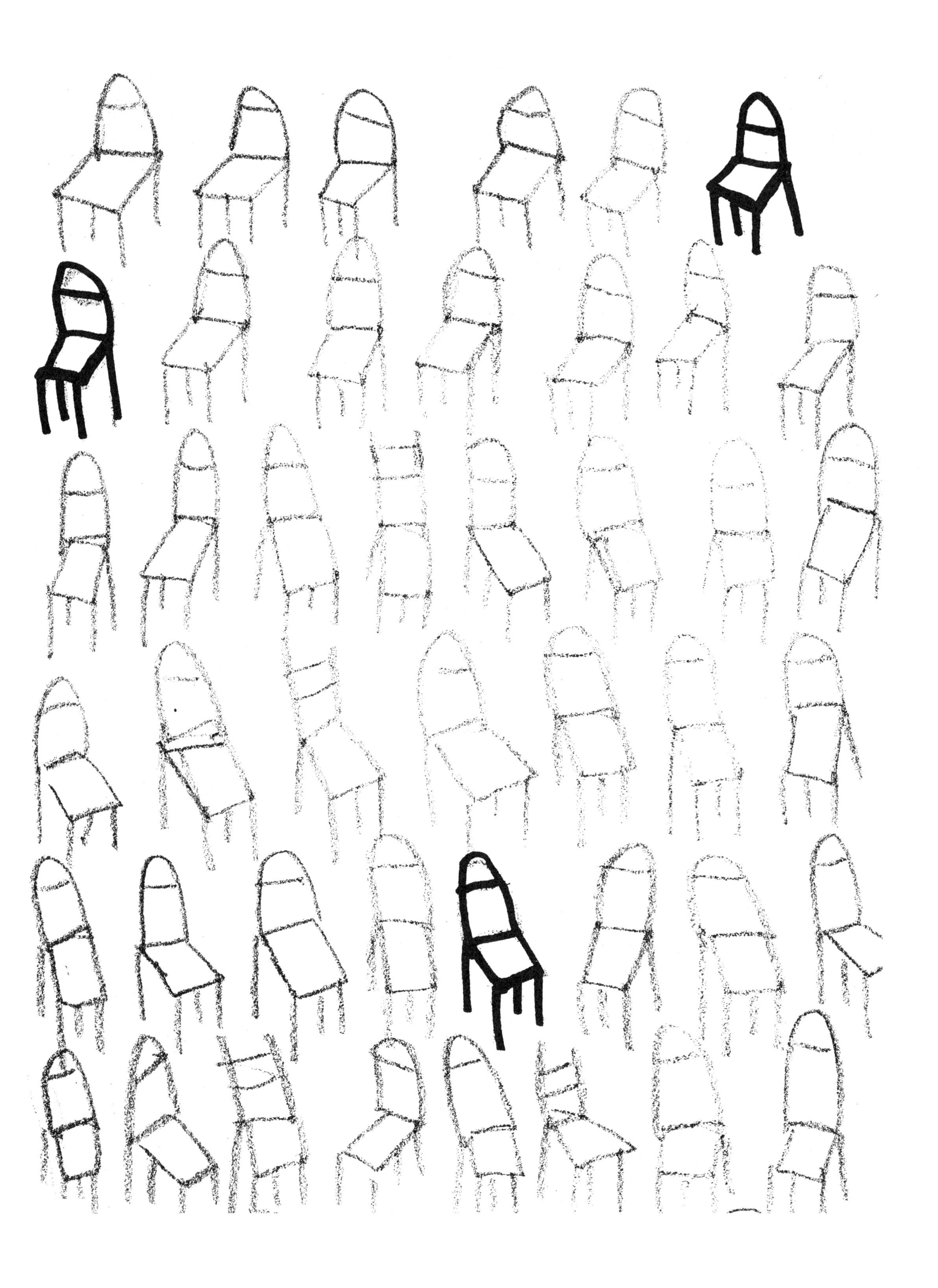

(NOTE: This script can be also be used for the 100 Musical Chairs—just adjust the numbers as described in the accompanying recipe.)

Prelude:	mmmmmmmm.......Money!
	Positions
	Conductor's Intro & Explanation
	Positions!!!
	Conductor Rehearses Audience
Movement 1:	Rant of the Rich
Movement 2:	Fortune and Misfortune
Movement 3:	Minimum Wage Blues
Movement 4:	American Dream Deferred
Movement 5:	Class War

Shorthand	Character
Conductor	Conductor
Upper Soloist	Upper Class Soloist
Middle Soloist 1	First Middle Class Soloist
Middle Soloist 2	Second Middle Class Soloist
Bottom Soloist 1	First Working Class Soloist
Bottom Soloist 2	Second Working Class Soloist
Upper	Upper Class Chorus (1 performer + 10% of audience)
Middle	Middle Class Chorus (4 performers + 40% of audience)
Bottom	Working Class Chorus (5 performers + 50% of audience)

Bold text in script indicates chorus lines that sections of the audience join in on.

PRELUDE

(On Conductor's signal)

Whole chorus: **mmmmmmmm.......Money!**

Conductor: Positions, everyone, positions...

(Performers take their 1976 positions: the Upper Soloist has 5 chairs to himself while the Middle and Working Class cram onto the other 5 chairs. Conductor addresses audience...)

Conductor: Ladies and gentlemen...good afternoon and welcome to our performance of the "10 Musical Chairs..."

[other introductory, welcoming remarks...]

Let us now begin the piece...

(Conductor turns to face performers, is dismayed at finding them in the 1976 arrangement, and turns back to address audience.)

Conductor: Indeed, you must excuse the chorus, they are still using the old score, based on information from 1976, in which the richest 10% of the population controlled 50% of the wealth, while the remaining 90% controlled the other 50%. However, much has changed in the last 20 years, and I have recently updated the score to reflect the current statistics—from 1997. I will now ask them to arrange themselves properly...

(Conductor turns to face performers...)

Conductor: Assume the position!

(Performers take their 1997 positions: the Upper Soloist has 7 chairs to himself while the Middle and Working Class cram onto the remaining 3 chairs. Conductor turns back to audience...)

Conductor: As a special treat for you today, we have decided to depart from the standard program and make this performance a little more "participatory." In this spirit, we have given out feather dusters to many of you...and bowler hats to a select few. We ask that you wave your feather dusters and tip your hats at the appropriate moments. We also ask that you join in on the choruses. Amongst you there are three choral groups: the upper class chorus, the shrinking middle class chorus, and the great working class chorus. Those of you on the line, tough luck! Now, let us rehearse your chants.

AUDIENCE REHEARSAL

(Conductor rehearses each of the choral groups, as follows:)

Upper	**I'm rich, you're not!**
Upper	**Trickle down.**
Middle & Bottom	**He's got more than all of us!**
Middle & Bottom	**Unfortunately...**
Middle	**Get a job!**
Bottom	**Got a job! It don't pay!**
Middle	**We can't buy a house!**
Bottom	**We can't pay the rent!**
Middle & Bottom	**Share the wealth!**
Conductor:	**Let us now begin the performance.**

MOVEMENT 1: Rant of the Rich

Whole chorus: **mmmmmmmm.......Money!**

(Upper Soloist swaggers his way along the chairs towards the center, addressing each group in turn.)

Upper Soloist: I am 10% of the US population.

I, all by my lonesome, control 70% of the wealth.

It's a tough job but somebody's gotta do it.

Now these pitiful, huddled vermin over here...represent a mere 90% of the U.S. population. They have 30% of the nation's wealth.

So what does this all mean...?

Well, basically, it comes down to this: I'm rich and they're not!

Or another way to look at it: They're not rich and I am!

But to put it simply: I'm stupendously bloated with wealth beyond human reason and they're fighting over my table scraps! And how, you might ask, does this make me feel? (pause) Yeooooow! It makes me feel good! I say, good!

(Upper Soloist does a strutting dance back to his 7 chairs, as he chants:)

Upper Soloist: I'm rich; you're not! I'm rich; you're not! I'm rich; you're not! I'm rich; you're not! I'm rich; you're not! I'm rich; you're not! I'm rich; you're not!

Upper: **I'm rich; you're not!**

Bottom & Middle: **He's got more than all of us!**

(Conductor brings the volume of the choruses up and down and up again as if the two choruses are battling against each other; Conductor then cuts them both off sharply.)

MOVEMENT 2: Fortune and Misfortune

Bottom Soloist 1: How did this happen, dammit?!!

Conductor: I'm glad you asked...
You see, during the last 20 years in the economic history of our nation...
The income of the bottom 60% declined, while the income of the richest 1% doubled.

Bottom & Middle: **Unfortunately...**

Upper Soloist: YOU are NOT in the richest 1%.

Conductor: While in a comparable period in the 50's and 60's, ALL segments of society saw EQUAL income gains.

Bottom & Middle: **Unfortunately...**

Upper Soloist: YOU are NOT living in the 1950's.

Conductor: While the buying power of the minimum wage fell to its lowest point since 1955, CEO salaries quadrupled. They now make 212 times the income of the average worker.

Bottom & Middle: **Unfortunately...**

Upper Soloist: YOU are NOT a CEO.

Conductor: When Thomas Frist was CEO of Hospital Corp of America, his salary was 127 million dollars a year. That's 60 thousand dollars an hour.

Bottom & Middle: **Unfortunately...**

Upper Soloist: YOU are NOT Thomas Frist.

Conductor: To finance the national debt, the government borrowed from the wealthy and now it pays them interest (with your tax dollars).

Bottom & Middle: **Unfortunately...**

Upper Soloist: The government did NOT borrow money from YOU.

Conductor: During the 1980's, the government cut taxes on the wealthy and waited for trickle down.

Bottom & Middle: **Unfortunately...**

Upper Soloist: YOU are still waiting.

Upper: **Trickle down.** (soft, up, down)

Bottom & Middle: **Share the wealth!** (soft, barely up, down)

MOVEMENT 3: Minimum Wage Blues

(Bottom Soloist 2 is in the kitchen, in the middle of a conversation with an imaginary conversation partner, her friend Carmen.)

Bottom Soloist 2: Listen, Carmen, this is getting serious, I've been looking for a job for 6 months and I can't find anything. I've got two years at the community college but the competition is just brutal... I don't know what I'm going to do.

Middle Soloist 1: Get a job! I'm sick and tired of you welfare queens layin' about, and snorting my taxes up your nose! Get a job!

Middle: **Get a job!**

(Chorus is strong and then cut off abruptly)

Bottom Soloist 1: I've got a job! In fact, I've got two jobs. But they're temporary and the wages are low. I've got a job but it don't pay!

Bottom: **Got a job! It don't pay!**

Middle: **Get a job!**

(Conductor brings the volume of the choruses up and down and up again as if the two choruses are battling against each other, then cuts them off sharply)

Upper Soloist: It works for ME.

[Bottom and Middle soloists should feel free to improvise around the lines above.]

MOVEMENT 4: American Dream Deferred

(Middle Soloist 2 slowly steps out towards audience, kneels down, places a bouquet of feather dusters gently on the ground beside an imaginary grave site.)

Middle Soloist 2: Hey gramps...it's me...Bobby. You know, I haven't been around in a while but I've been thinking a lot lately about how things must have been for you. I don't know how you did it. You came over, with just a suitcase...and somehow, you made it happen. You did it. First the Laundromat, then the clothing store, and then the dry-cleaning business. But gramps, it's just not like that anymore, I don't know why. You put dad through school—I gotta pay for my education for the next 20 years. Sally and I are both working. Working really hard. We're running like crazy just to stay in place. I haven't seen the kids in weeks. We'd like to settle down in a nice neighborhood, raise the kids, and buy a small house. I want that American Dream. But I can't buy a house. I can't even buy a house.

Middle: **We can't buy a house!**

(Conductor starts chorus at medium volume, then brings it down to a whisper and cuts it off.)

(Bottom Soloist 2 comes towards audience and engages an invisible conversation partner.) (During the story about her landlord demanding the rent, she plays out both sides of the confrontation, beginning more campy and shocked and ending more serious and defiant.)

Bottom Soloist 2: I don't know...this is the last straw, I mean, the roof leaks, the door knobs come off...I saw a rat in 'Millio's crib last week. And, can you believe it, yesterday, he raises the rent...what a scene it was...he just comes right in and says, "You must pay the rent!" and I say, "But I can't pay the rent!"...and he says..."You must pay the rent!" and then I say to him again, "But I can't pay the rent!"...and again he says..."You must pay the rent!" and of course I say, "But I can't pay the rent!"

Bottom: **We can't pay the rent!**

Middle: **We can't buy a house!**

(In turn, Conductor brings each chorus up and then down to a whisper; he then brings them both up together and cuts them off sharply.)

Bottom Soloist 2: YOU can't buy A HOUSE?

Middle Soloist 2: YOU can't pay THE RENT?

Upper Soloist: It works for ME.

MOVEMENT 5: Class War

Upper: **Trickle down!**

Bottom & Middle: **Share the wealth!**

(This is a quick set of choruses. Conductor begins with "Trickle down!," then has "Share the wealth!" roar up fast and end strong.)

(Then Upper Soloist and the Bottom and Middle performers exchange the following lines in a call and response fashion.)

Upper Soloist:	Bottom & Middle:
Go away!	**Have our say!**
Don't make trouble!	**Burst the bubble!**
Borrowed 'n spent!	**Can't pay the rent!**
Dirty louse!	**Can't buy a house!**
Welfare cheat!	**Gotta eat!**
Communist!	**We are pissed!**
Please don't shout!	**What's it about?!**
Up the ladder!	**Things that matter!**
Swimming pools!	**Fixing schools!**
Leisure time!	**Five and Dime!**
Making deals!	**Eating meals!**
Man 'o the hour!	**We want power!**
Living large!	**Let's take charge!**
Downsize!	**Organize!**

("Organize!" is the loudest line, and as they say it, Bottom and Middle all stand up together, with their feather dusters in the air. And then go right into the last chant:)

Bottom & Middle: **Share the wealth!**

(Conductor brings chorus up from whisper to crescendo, cranking it up a couple notches higher than any previous chant, then cuts it off and bows. All bow.)

100 MUSICAL CHAIRS

Complete Recipe

Description

100 Musical Chairs is a large-scale participatory performance that dramatizes the growing disparity between the very rich and everyone else. 100 chairs (each representing 1% of the US wealth) are arranged in a wide arc. 100 participants (each representing 1% of the US population) sit on the chairs in a series of "human bar graphs" that portray with statistical accuracy the increasingly unequal distribution of US wealth. (In the final 1997 arrangement, the richest 1% occupies 40 chairs, the next richest 9 people sit comfortably in the middle 30 chairs, and the remaining 90 people pile on top of each other in the remaining 30 chairs.)

While in these sculptures, participants are led by a conductor, dressed in full tuxedo and tails, through a five-movement chanted choral performance, complete with soloists, and sections representing the working, middle and upper classes.

100 Musical Chairs can be performed indoors at union conventions, activist conferences, and school assemblies as well as outdoors at festivals, or rallies. (Those of you who have participated in United for a Fair Economy's popular education workshop, will recognize the 100 Musical Chairs as a dramatization of our "10 Chairs" role play.)

Mr. So and So kicks back with his 40% of the wealth while private security keeps a close eye on troublemakers. Kosta Demos and Kevin Leppmann at City Hall Plaza, Boston, October, 1995. *photo Laura Wulf*

How to Prepare

10 Chairs or 100 Chairs? If you're not sure whether the 10 Musical Chairs or the 100 Musical Chairs (see previous recipe) is more appropriate for your needs, consider the following summary of their similarities and differences. They apply the same concept and use virtually the same script. The 100 Musical Chairs is 10 times bigger, quite a bit more spectacular, involves more people in a more physical way, shows a higher level of statistical detail, but requires a lot more room and is a lot more complicated to set up, perform and break down.

In general, the 10 Musical Chairs gives you more for your dollar. We also recommend it for all indoor settings other than school gymnasiums or the like. The 100 Musical Chairs is best done outside, on a college green, for example, and in settings where the media attention you can leverage from the sheer extraordinary size and spectacle of it makes it worth the extra effort.

Choosing a venue. Space must be quite large. The voices of far away soloists must travel well. 50-100 volunteers must be available. Because when the piece works well, it can get very loud, choose a venue where this is not a problem.

Obtaining props. Feather dusters can be purchased at Woolworth's, departments stores, local hardware stores...etc. for approximately $1.50/per. However, it is unlikely

INGREDIENTS -- 100 MUSICAL CHAIRS

	gourmet 	homestyle 	microwave 
space:	200 ft long semicircle	200 ft long semicircle	200 ft long semicircle
performance time:	15-25 minutes	15-25 minutes	15-20 minutes
set up time:	4 person hours	3 person hours	2 person hours
prep time:	5 hours*	3 hours*	1/2 hour*
performers:			
heavily involved	1	1	1
modestly involved	5	3	
lightly involved	95	97	100
helpers:	3-4	1-2	1-2
props:	script**	script**	script**
	100 number signs	100 number signs	100 number signs
	100 location tickets	100 location tickets	100 location tickets
	1 conductor's tux	1 conductor's tux	1 black suit
	appropriate clothing		
	100 chairs	100 chairs	100 chairs
	90+ feather dusters	3-5 feather dusters	
	10+ bowler hats	1 bowler hat	1 bowler or shades
Notes on versions	Use a full 5 soloists, one for each part in the script. Have soloists wear clothing appropriate to their social class. Rehearse well, particularly the solos in movement 4 and the call and response in movement 5.	Piece can be handily done with just 3 soloists. Have the middle class soloist play both middle class solo parts, likewise, have the working class soloist play both working class solo parts. Have bowler hats and feather dusters for the soloists but not the mass of volunteers.	Performance can be done quick and dirty. Label only every 5th or 10th chair. Drop movement 4 from the script. Instead of memorizing lines, participants can read from the scripts during the performance. If necessary, soloists can be found as little as 1/2 hour before the performance and pressed into service. Also, the piece can be performed effectively with minimal or no props: Use a black suit of some kind in place of the conductor's tux. Any kind of hat or dark sunglasses will work for the richest 1%. Forget the feather dusters. (Also, if chairs are a problem, try reworking the performance around cans of soup or books or the like.)

*Does not include Conductor's prep time.

**Use script for 10 Musical Chairs, supplied with previous recipe.

you will find more than 20, never mind 90+, in any one place. Stores will order them in bulk if you arrange it. Give enough time for delivery and work out a wholesale discount. Also, buy one extra that is especially elegant, the conductor can use it as a baton.

Bowler hats can be purchased at local costume or joke shops. The low-end versions go for about $7/per. A conductor's tux can be rented from any tux shop for about $65. Also, in any major city, there should be at least one store that sells used tuxes where you might be able to pick up a full outfit for about $125. Thus, if you are doing performances on two or more separate days, it might pay to buy.

Chairs. Any chairs will do but the chairs that work best are sturdy, narrow, easy to move, and have no arms. Some institutional-style chairs snap together and this can help increase stability. It is visually stronger if all the chairs are the same shape and color, preferably black. In any case, **you must have exactly 100 chairs**—no more and no less.

Setting up the chairs. Setting up the chairs can be quite a feat of civil engineering. To be safe, you will need a couple of volunteers and a full hour to set up. If the space is big enough (likely, if performed outside; unlikely, if inside), arrange the chairs in a single long, gentle arc (see stage layout diagram #1). (An arc is much better than a straight line because it creates a focusing effect and allows all participants to see each other.) Since the average chair is 18 inches wide, this geometry requires an arc of approximately 150 ft in circumference.

If constrained by a smaller space, you can double or triple up chairs in concentric arcs (see stage layout diagram #2). It is also possible to combine these options by doubling up on the left side, for example, where only a few people will be scattered, while keeping the chairs in a single line on the right side, where many people will be piled on (see stage layout diagram #3).

Also, if using a multiple-row arrangement, it is advisable to leave breaks in the front rows so participants can more easily reach the chairs in the back rows when they must change seats. In general, it helps to place the widest and sturdiest of your chairs in the rightmost locations, as these will have to bear the greatest load.

Numbering the chairs. It is essential to number the chairs. Prior to the day of the performance, create 100 signs, numbered 1-100. (Use half of an 8 1/2 x 11 sheet of paper and either a thick magic marker or a big computer font.) Then, on the day of the performance, AFTER you have arranged your chairs, attach one number sign to each chair, with #1 on the leftmost chair and #100 on the rightmost.

Tape the sheet to the front of the chair, just below the lip of the seat (here it won't get crushed or dislodged and can still be easily seen). Before actually attaching any number signs to the chairs, it is advisable to check that you have exactly 100 chairs properly arranged. A good way to do this is to go around to all the chairs and lay the numbers out on the seats you plan to attach them to. If all numbers are accounted for, then you're set and ready to tape them on.

In addition, if you are using a chair arrangement with more than one row (see above, "setting up the chairs"), you may find yourself uncertain exactly how to number the chairs. It is important to number from left to right as much as possible. So, for example, if you had two concentric rows of 50 chairs, you would NOT number one row 1-50 and then the other row 51-100 because that would put chair 51 right behind chair 1. You want to number the chairs by going back and forth from row to row as you proceed from left to right so that chair 2 ends up just behind chair 1 and chair 100 just behind chair 99. This is not a detail, it is essential for building a visually clear economic sculpture once participants start taking their chair positions. (See stage diagrams #'s 1-3.)

How to Serve

The Conductor. The conductor is the linchpin of the 100 Musical Chairs. If he (or she) is well prepared and practiced, then the piece will work, no matter how well everything else comes together. His secret is that, while disguised as a formal conductor, he is elegantly directing, stage managing and MCing the whole show right as it happens. He is able to begin, end and modulate all the choruses, orchestrate a raw audience, and cue ill-prepared soloists—all from within the show, without anyone noticing or caring. This is why the microwave version can work so well with so little other preparation.

ticket # 47
BEGIN in chair # **72**
In **1976** go to chair # **85**
In **1997** go to chair # **91**

Chair assignments. Chair assignment tickets are essential. The tickets tell participants which chair to sit on at the beginning of the piece and which chairs to move to as the piece unfolds.

As mentioned earlier, the chair assignments only work when there are exactly 100 chairs, properly arranged and properly numbered (as described in "How to Prepare", above). A list of the chair assignments are included with this recipe but you need to turn them into tickets. Tickets should be numbered and color coded as indicated and always be given out to participants, in order, beginning with ticket #1. Why? The ticket order is cleverly designed to create an even distribution regardless of how many people end up participating. Thus, if only 70 people show up to the event or are willing to participate, the absolute numbers won't be correct, but the proportions will be and the overall visual effect will still look right.

Although 100 participants is ideal, with 75 the difference is barely noticeable once the piece gets going, and even with 50 the piece works reasonably well. Remember, though: **EVERYONE who participates MUST be assigned to a chair and thus MUST receive a ticket**. Note that the first few tickets are earmarked for the soloists.

Gathering volunteers into the performance. You will need to gather a large number of volunteers into the performance just before it begins. Let's assume you are performing in a venue with a relatively captive audience (school assembly, conference plenary, indoor special event...etc.).

Identify 2-4 volunteer "ushers" to help out. Deputize one usher as your captain and give her the chair assignment tickets. Make sure she understands

that she needs to give them out in order, starting with the lowest ticket number not already assigned to a soloist (see above). For this reason, the tickets should NOT be broken into piles.

The other ushers should be given the feather dusters and bowler hats and instructed to follow her lead. As each person enters the hall, the captain should ask them if they wish to participate, and if so, give them the next ticket in the stack. If the ticket is white (upper class), the volunteer should get a bowler hat. If the ticket is blue (middle class) or red (working class), the volunteer should get a feather duster. Volunteers should then be told to go sit in the seat indicated by "Begin at seat #..." on their ticket.

These instructions should be adjusted for outdoor settings where it may be considerably more difficult to gather a critical mass of volunteers and corral them into the piece.

How to "sit" on the chairs. For most of the performance, 90 people have to find a way to sit on 30 chairs. Some people feel uncomfortable sitting in a stranger's lap, while for others it's a hoot. Others, such as the elderly, disabled, or very large people, may have more physical concerns. Encourage participants to be sensitive to these differences but also to relax and have fun.

Unlike the 10 Chairs, in the 100 Chairs, you can't shape a certain look by controlling how participants physically sit in their assigned chairs. So don't try too hard. Just let it happen.

"Share the wealth! Share the wealth!" Feather dusters in hand, the majority demands justice during the *100 Musical Chairs* at City Hall Plaza, Boston, October, 1995. *photo Laura Wulf*

One simple rule that helps to structure things is to tell everyone they must be "on" a chair in some way (i.e. not simply standing behind it or sitting in front of it).

Tips and Tricks for the Conductor. You should play the Conductor big and with a lot of authority. Use physical humor. Play off the audience and

improvise. During the choruses, some one will often trail off after everyone else has cut off. You can get a lot of laughs out of these moments, by shooting them a look or making an off-hand comment. Come up with your own one-liners. You might encourage the Middle Class to get louder with their "Get a job!" chant, by saying, "Come on Middle Class, this is your mantra!" Or you might encourage the Working class to use their feather dusters, by saying, "Wave those feather dusters! Whaddya think they are? The hammer and sickle of the service economy?!" Think about your entrance. Be dramatic but clear with your conducting signals. Use the video as a guide.

Rehearsing the audience. At the appropriate time in the performance (see page 3 of attached script), the conductor will identify sections of the audience by class and instruct them on how to join in on the choruses, etc. The rehearsal can actually be one of the richest and most fun moments in the piece because it foreshadows the whole performance and it is the moment when the audience is first really getting into the act. It is the key moment for establishing a good bond with the audience.

Spice to Taste

Encourage the performers to improvise. The Upper Class Soloist might embellish his lines with ranting and raving or add more complexity to his character by showing some doubt or anxiety or guilt. The middle and working class soloists might adapt their lines to better reflect the images and language of their own lives.

Backdrop. Paint a banner with a slogan or a mural-like visual story and place it behind the 100 chairs for the performance.

Customize the script. Write a new movement, complete with its own chorus lines and solos, that addresses the particular issues and concerns of your audience. Add it in to the middle or use it in place of an existing movement (movement 4 is a good one to replace).

Machine. Build a "machine" that replaces the role of ushers in a more theatrical way. To enter the performance, volunteers pass through the machine where they receive "class identities" (including chair assignment tickets and props). For one of our outdoor performances, we built a multi-station machine which integrated cardboard backdrops, human actors, and recorded sound. For ideas on how to get started on building your own machine, look at the "Engines of Inequality" theater game in "Chapter 3: Soup to Nuts."

Costume/Giant Puppets. Experiment with various masks or larger than life costumes for the soloists. Or create a giant puppet that represents the Richest 1% and gradually spreads out across his share of the chairs as the piece proceeds. Or create an inflatable costume for the Richest 1% so that he can be pumped up and grow more and more bloated as his wealth increases.

Fool. Add a silent Fool character, who moves about the performance, buffooning and counterpointing in various ways: 1) cleans the Richest 1%'s chairs with a feather duster; 2) tiptoes across the Richest 1%'s chairs, while trying to count them on her fingers but loses count and has to start over; 3) tries to elbow her way into the 90% but finds it too crowded and is thrown back

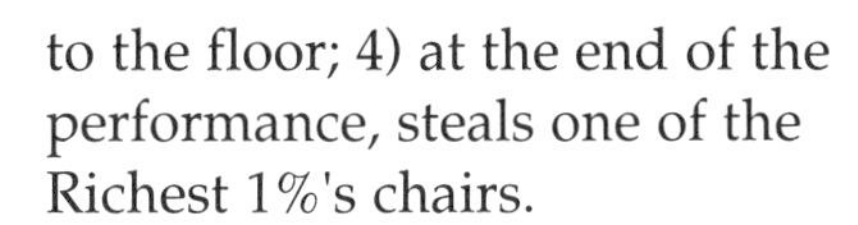

Conductor and Fool and a whole lot of chairs. David Behrstock and Andrew Boyd in the 100 Musical Chairs, Copley Square, Boston, October, 1995. *photo Marilyn Humphries*

to the floor; 4) at the end of the performance, steals one of the Richest 1%'s chairs.

Additional Resources Available

Video. A video of the 100 Chairs is available from United for a Fair Economy. The video can help in a multitude of ways: generating interest, deciding whether it is an appropriate action for you, learning the exact rhythms of the chants, imagining how to arrange things spatially, etc. It is highly recommended. ($10)

Translation. A full Spanish translation of the script and a partial Haitian Creole translation are also available. (free)

Complete Action Kit. Everything you need to do the gourmet version of the 100 Chairs (except the tuxedo), including: video, 10 bowler hats, 100 feather dusters, 100 chair number signs, 100 location tickets, etc. (inquire as to price).

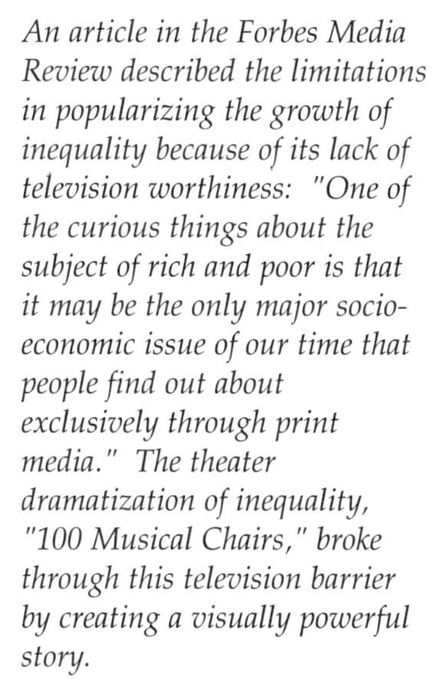

An article in the Forbes Media Review described the limitations in popularizing the growth of inequality because of its lack of television worthiness: "One of the curious things about the subject of rich and poor is that it may be the only major socio-economic issue of our time that people find out about exclusively through print media." The theater dramatization of inequality, "100 Musical Chairs," broke through this television barrier by creating a visually powerful story.

—United for a Fair Economy, Annual Report, 1996

INFO SHEET -- 100 MUSICAL CHAIRS

CHAIR ASSIGNMENT CHART

TICKET NUMBER	CLASS	START	1976	1997	NOTES
1	U	1	11	21	Richest 1%
2	M	33	63	78	Middle Soloist #1
3	W	78	88	93	Lower Soloist #1
4	M	44	69	82	Middle Soloist #2
5	W	67	82	89	Lower Soloist #2
6	M	16	54	72	
7	W	89	94	97	
8	M	28	60	76	
9	W	62	79	88	
10	U	5	32	52	
11	M	39	67	80	
12	W	73	85	91	
13	M	50	73	84	
14	W	84	92	95	
15	M	14	53	72	
16	W	95	98	99	
17	M	19	55	73	
18	W	59	78	87	
19	M	25	59	75	
20	U	10	47	67	
21	W	65	81	89	
22	M	31	62	77	
23	W	70	84	90	
24	M	36	65	79	
25	W	76	87	92	
26	M	42	58	75	
27	W	81	90	94	
28	M	47	71	83	
29	W	87	93	96	
30	U	3	26	46	
31	M	53	74	85	
32	W	92	96	98	
33	M	13	52	71	
34	W	98	99	100	
35	M	15	53	72	
36	W	58	77	86	
37	M	18	55	73	
38	W	61	79	87	
39	M	21	57	74	
40	U	7	38	58	
41	W	64	80	88	
42	M	24	58	75	
43	W	66	82	89	
44	M	27	60	76	
45	W	69	83	90	
46	M	30	62	77	
47	W	72	85	91	
48	M	32	63	78	
49	W	75	87	92	
50	U	2	23	43	
51	M	35	64	79	
52	W	77	88	93	
53	M	38	66	80	
54	W	80	89	94	
55	M	41	68	81	
56	W	83	91	95	
57	M	43	69	81	
58	W	86	93	96	
59	M	46	70	82	
60	U	9	44	64	
61	W	88	94	96	
62	M	49	72	83	
63	W	91	95	97	
64	M	52	74	84	
65	W	94	97	98	
66	M	54	75	85	
67	W	97	99	99	
68	M	17	54	73	
69	W	99	100	100	
70	U	6	35	55	
71	M	20	56	74	
72	W	57	77	86	
73	M	23	58	75	
74	W	60	78	87	
75	M	26	59	76	
76	W	63	80	88	
77	M	29	61	77	
78	W	68	83	90	
79	M	34	64	78	
80	U	8	41	61	
81	W	71	84	91	
82	M	37	65	79	
83	W	74	86	92	
84	M	40	67	80	
85	W	79	89	93	
86	M	45	70	82	
87	W	82	90	94	
88	M	48	72	83	
89	W	85	92	95	
90	U	4	29	49	
91	M	51	73	84	
92	W	90	95	97	
93	M	55	75	85	
94	W	93	97	98	
95	M	11	51	71	
96	W	96	98	99	
97	M	22	57	74	
98	W	56	76	86	
99	M	12	52	71	
100	W	100	100	100	

Use this chart to make chair assignment tickets as described in accompanying recipe.

"U" = Upper Class; color coded White.
"M" = Middle Class, color coded Blue.
"W" = Working Class; color coded Red.

Resources of various kinds that will keep you cooking for a long time to come.

Manuals & Guidebooks

Culture Jamming: Hacking, Slashing and Sniping in the Empire of Signs, Mark Dery, Open Magazine Pamphlet Series, Open Media, 1993. $4. P.O. Box 2726 Westfield, NJ 07091. 908/789-9608. Excellent pamphlet. *The* manifesto for culture jammers.

A Troublemaker's Handbook: How to Fight Back Where You Work—and Win!, Dan LaBotz. 350pgs. $17 + $3 shipping. Labor Notes. 7435 Michigan Ave. Detroit, MI 48210. 313/842-6262. A wide ranging compendium of stories of workers fighting back creatively in their workplaces.

Billboard Liberation Front Manual (excerpt from Processed World #25, Summer/Fall 1990, pps 22-6, San Francisco, CA). A basic guide to the art and science of billboard correcting—by the experts.

Playing Boal: Games for Actors and Non-Actors, Augusto Boal, Routledge Press, London, 1992. A comprehensive resource packed with hundreds of theater games to stimulate the senses and the imagination. Each game described in full.

Organizing for Social Change: A Manual for Activists in the 1990's, Kim Bobo, Midwest Academy, 1991. $19.95. 225 W. Ohio, Suite 250, Chicago, IL 60610. 312/645-6010. Comprehensive organizer's manual in the Alinsky tradition. Good sections on designing actions and using the media. Strong focus on direct action tactics and how they serve strategic campaigns—provides a helpful balancing for the cookbook in this area.

War Resisters League Organizer's Manual, Ed Hedemann, Ed., War Resisters League, 1981. $6. War Resisters League, 339 Lafayette St., New York, NY, 10012. A comprehensive organizers manual. Useful chapters on street theater, street fairs, and designing leaflets.

...art is not something you can carry up to an East Side Manhattan apartment in an elevator.

—JAMES TURRELL

Poetry, like bread, is for everyone.

—OTTO RENE CASTILLO

The Lesbian Avenger Handbook: A Handy Guide to Homemade Revolution, Lesbian Avengers, 1993. c/o The Center, 208 W. 13th St. New York, NY, 10011. 212/967-7711x3204. A cut to the chase manual with attitude. A guide to direct action and guerrilla media, Avenger-style. Lots of good tips on designing leaflets, wheat-pasting and working the media.

Let the World Know: Make Your Cause News, Jason Salzman, Rocky Mountain Media Watch, 1995. $10. P.O. Box 18858, Denver, CO 80218. 303/832-7558. A clear and concise guide to the media for social activists. Strong section on visual and theatrical stunts from which a number of examples featured in the cookbook were drawn.

How to Tell and Sell your Story: A Guide to Media for Community Groups and Other NonProfits, Community Change, Issue 18, Winter 1997. $7 (less for more copies). Center for Community Change, 1000 Wisconsin Ave., NW, Washington, DC, 20007. 202/342-0567. Handy guide to the media for social activists.

ROAR: The Paper Tiger Television Guide to Media Activism, Daniel Marcus, Ed., Paper Tiger Television Collective, 1991. 339 Lafayette St., New York, NY, 10012. A handy guide to media literacy, the new wave of camcorder activism and the nuts and bolts of low-budget community video.

68 Ways to Make Really Big Puppets, Sarah Peatie, Bread & Puppet Press/Troll Press, St. Johnsbury, 1996. Pupeteers Cooperative, 181 Tremont, Somerville MA, 02143. The nuts and bolts of spectacle. Everything from how to attach cloth to a pole to how to build a multi-articulated dragon a city-block long. Probably, the ultimate resource on large puppet making.

Wise Fool Basics: A Handbook of Our Core Techniques, K. Ruby, Wise Fool Puppets, San Francisco, 1992. Easy to follow technical instructions on how to construct puppets, masks, stilts, etc.

Books

But is it Art? : The Spirit of Art as Activism, Nina Felshin, Ed., Bay Press, Seattle, 1995. $18.95. 206/284-5913. A superb series of essays about activist art and artful action that chronicle the history of WAC, Guerrilla Girls, Gran Fury, and ACT-UP, among others. Excellent companion to the cookbook.

Reimaging America: The Arts of Social Change, Mark O'Brien & Craig Little, Eds., New Society Publishers, Philadelphia, 1990. An interesting survey of political artists and community oriented cultural projects. Maybe out of print—politely call editor at 718/789-4407 to locate a copy.

Street Theater and Other Outdoor Performance, Bim Mason, Routeledge, London and New York, 1992. Great exploration of the contemporary street theater scene in Europe. Section on "Ways and means," was a great help in writing parts of Chapter 3: Soup to Nuts in the cookbook.

Disturbing the Peace: 20th Century Radical Street Performance, Jan Cohen-Cruz, Ed. forthcoming from Routledge Press, London & New York, Spring, 1998. A deep exploration of how radical movements have creatively used public space throughout the century and throughout the world.

AIDS Demo Graphics, Douglas Crimp with Adam Rolston, Bay Press, Seattle, 1990. $13.95. 206/284-5913. A collection of ACT-UP's best graphics and a chronicle of its major actions. Great visuals.

Pranks! : Devious Deeds and Mischievous Mirth, RE/Search #11, RE/Search Publications, 1987. $17.99. 20 Romolo #B, San Francisco, CA 94133. 415/771-7117. Truly a one of a kind resource: A compendium of the most outrageous political and artistic pranks of the last three decades.

Magazines

AdBusters Magazine / The Media Foundation. Quarterly magazine of culture jamming, anti-advertising, and "the mental environment." Superb graphics. Great website. If you hate advertising sleaze, you must get AdBusters. Call for free "Culture Jamming on Campus" action kit. To order, call 800/663-1243. Check out web site at www.adbusters.com.

High Performance Magazine / Art in the Public Interest. Monthly magazine of community performance and socially engaged art. API also provides resources, workshops, support, and networking for cultural workers and groups. P.O. Box 68, Saxapahaw, NC 27340. 910/376-8404. Well organized web site: www.artswire.org/highperf

Organizations & Networks

Labor Heritage Foundation. The central hub in an extensive labor cultural network of musicians, storytellers, muralists, etc. Well organized; great people. Organizes inspiring and delightful national labor arts exchange every June (3rd weekend). Suite 301, 815 16th St., N.W., Washington, DC 20006. 202/842-7880.

Northland Poster Collective. A graphic production collective in Minneapolis that custom produces posters, buttons, bumperstickers, etc. for the national labor movement for more than a decade.

Alliance for Cultural Democracy. National network of cultural activists. 415/437-2721.

Cultural Workers Action Committee. CWAC (logo is a duck brandishing a paint brush), is a group of cultural workers linked to the new Labor Party. Contact Mike Alewitz at: 908/220-1472. email: lamp@igc.apc.org.

Labor Action Mural Project. Like what the name says, organized by muralist extraordinaire, Mike Alewitz. 908/220-1472. email: lamp@igc.apc.org.

Center for the Theater of the Oppressed in Omaha. The central hub of the Theater of the Oppressed in the US. Contact: Doug Paterson, Department of Dramatic Arts, Fine Arts Building, University of Nebraska, Omaha NE 68182. 402/554-2422. paterson@fa-cpacs.unomaha.edu

The Applied and Interactive Theater Guide. A gateway to a vast range of interactive theater resources on the web. http://csep.suny-it.edu/~joel/guide.html (that's right, no "www" in this address).

Guerrilla Groups

Guerrilla Media Collective. Check out this superb and inspiring website, filled with examples of a few of the most sophisticated guerrilla media exploits in North America. Particularly useful is an extensive how to guide for doing your own newspaper wraps. http://mindlink.bc.ca/gmedia (that's right, no "www").

Guerrilla Girls. The "conscience of the art world" is on line. Check out the website of these media savvy guerrilla gorillas. www.voyagerco.com/gg/gg.html

Theater Groups

Bread & Puppet Theater. Puppets, spectacles, and processions for social justice for over 30 years. Sublime and elemental. RD2, P.O. Box 153, Glover, VT 05839. 802/525-3031.

San Francisco Mime Troupe. Great campy melodrama for social justice for over 30 years. 855 Treat St., San Francisco, CA 94110. 415/285-1717.

Films

Yippie! Showcases some of the guerrilla theater techniques developed by Abbie Hoffman and friends during the 60's. Available from 3rd World Newsreel in New York. 212/947-9277.

Sonic Outlaws. Craig Baldwin. Explores creative resistance to the mass media in the 90's. Looks at pirate radio, camcorder activism, collage, billboard correction, and fair use law. Includes footage of the Barbie Liberation Front in action.

To search for the good and make it matter: this is the real challenge for the artist.

—Estrella Conwill Májozo

We hope the ideas, tools and perspectives showcased in this cookbook will not only inspire great creative actions, but also continue to build the Art for a Fair Economy community—a growing national network of artists and activists seeking creative ways to reach people and challenge the cultural myths that support economic inequality.

ART FOR A FAIR ECONOMY

The Art for a Fair Economy project in Boston serves as a national clearinghouse for creative work around economic inequality, offering ideas, information, resources, and assistance. If you are using the cookbook in your work and have questions or need help of any kind, contact us.

If you want to link up with other people in your area (in local collaboratives, street theater troupes, etc.), we may be able to put you in touch and help get you started. If you undertake an action or come up with new and useful ideas, pass them along. Periodic updates to the cookbook will include new recipes and action ideas developed by people, like yourself, who are using the cookbook in the field. To assist in these efforts we provide the following resources:

Newsletter and Listserve. Through our newsletter and internet listserve (an electronic mailing list), participants stay in touch, share ideas and experiences, and collaborate on projects. To subscribe to the newsletter, mail or call us at the address below. To subscribe to the listserve just send an email message to stw@stw.org, asking to be put on the Art for a Fair Economy listserve. Our listserve is usually moderated, which means all messages sent to the list are first reviewed before being sent on to the entire membership of the list. This filters out junk, helps keep exchanges on target and allows for some editorial control.

Creative Action Workshops. We offer hands-on training workshops built around the cookbook, that demonstrate successful street theater and guerrilla media techniques, walk participants through a design process for devising their own actions, and offer strategies for opening the culture to the agenda of economic equality. We also offer workshops specifically geared to train participants to perform the 10 and 100 Musical Chairs, including rehearsals, and a step-by-step walk-through of the entire event planning process.

Performances. If you're not quite ready to put on your own performances, you can invite our Boston-based theater troupe, Class Acts, to perform at your union, school, or conference. Our repertoire includes most of the action-performances described in the cookbook—-and more!

Poster Nation. As mentioned in the cuisines section, Poster Nation is a coordinated nationwide postering campaign organized by United for a Fair Economy. On a few key days each year (Tax Day, Labor Day, Election Day, etc.), activists post a similar set of posters in public places all over the country. The campaign is coordinated in an open-ended, decentralized fashion over the Internet. The Poster Nation web page (www.stw.org/posters) allows you to join the campaign, view and download any of the current posters, offer new posters of your own invention, as well as locate other people in your area who are active in the campaign.

Additional Materials and Merchandise. We offer a range of additional resources, including: books, posters, buttons, stickers, cassette tapes, videos, and organizing kits—all for the fight against economic inequality. Contact us for a current resource list.

UNITED FOR A FAIR ECONOMY

United for a Fair Economy (formerly "Share the Wealth") draws public attention to the dangerous consequences of growing income and wealth inequality—and points the way toward solutions. Through popular education programs, research, advocacy and theater, we are closing the widening gap between the very wealthy and everyone else.

Contact us and get involved—join our economics education network, lead workshops about economic inequality and help build a fair economy. We also have information on timely legislation to cut corporate welfare, close the wage gap, and restore fairness to our tax system. Our programs include:

Popular Economics Education. We have designed dozens of engaging and participatory economics education programs that have been widely disseminated. In 1996, we did about 500 workshops for over 15,000 people in unions, community groups and religious congregations. We now staff a national volunteer economics educators network with hundreds of members. Our workshops are easy to conduct and we're committed to training hundreds more people to feel confident delivering the message.

Tools for Organizing. We have worked directly with constituency groups to

Let me give you a word on the philosophy of reform. The whole history of the progress of human liberty shows that all concessions yet made to her august claims have been born of earnest struggle. The conflict has been exciting, agitating, all absorbing, and for the time being putting all other tumults to silence. It must do this or it does nothing. If there is no struggle, there is no progress. Those who profess to favor freedom, and yet deprecate agitation, are men who want crops without plowing up the ground. They want rain without thunder and lightning. They want the ocean without the awful roar of its many waters. This struggle may be a moral one; or it may be a physical one; or it may be both moral and physical; but it must be a struggle. Power concedes nothing without a demand. It never did and it never will. Find out just what people will submit to, and you have found the exact amount of injustice and wrong which will be imposed upon them; and these will continue until they are resisted with either words or blows, or with both. The limits of tyrants are prescribed by the endurance of those whom they oppress.

—FREDERICK DOUGLASS

While there is a lower class I am in it.

While there is a criminal element I am of it

While there is a soul in prison I am not free.

—EUGENE V. DEBS

develop tools to fight back against attacks. Things like "corporate welfare talking points" for welfare activists, organizing kits, and posters. We co-publish a quarterly newsletter full of factoids, humorous articles and information about inequality that other groups and individuals draw on for their publications.

Creative Action. Most people know they are getting robbed, but feel hopeless and can't see any alternative. Early on, we found that humor, theater and creative approaches are a key ingredient in getting people involved in the fight against inequality. We started a theater group, Class Acts, that is now being hired as entertainment at political conferences and union conventions throughout the US and Canada. This cookbook is a natural continuation of that work.

Example moves the world more than doctrine.

—HENRY MILLER

Action Campaigns. We staff a national coalition of about 250 unions and political groups working on "A Campaign To Close the Wage Gap." At the center of this is legislation to raise the minimum wage to a living wage and deny corporations the right to deduct top salaries in excess of 25 times the lowest paid worker in a firm. We like this approach because it introduces the concept of a "wage ratio" as a principle for collective bargaining, giving or denying tax breaks, and other arrangements.

Research. UFE focuses on translating existing research into tools for organizing. Last fall we issued an original study about the sources of wealth of the Forbes 400 because we kept running up against the "bootstrap" mythology that "anyone in America can get rich." Our study, "Born on Third Base," revealed in 1997 that over 70% of the Forbes 400 were born into the richest 2% of households. Over 43% inherited their way directly onto the list, with wealth exceeding $400 million dollars. Some Horatio Alger story!

Responsible Wealth. We're organizing business leaders and well known wealthy people to speak up in the media against the way "the rules of our economy are skewed to favor the rich."

Media Work. We've enlisted many of our popular educators to be part of a rapid response team who write letters to the editor, get on talk radio and become local sources and experts on economic fairness issues.

We're still a shoe-string operation: solid as a rock and hanging by a thread. But what the hey, you just can't sit back sometimes. Besides, we're having a helluva lot of fun. We'd love to hear from you.

If you're interested, here's some things you can do:

- Join United for a Fair Economy for $25 per year and receive our quarterly newsletter Too Much, timely action alerts and much more.
- Link up with Art for a Fair Economy.
- Contribute your own ideas, recipes or graphics to become part of our website, posters, and periodic cookbook updates.
- Invite us to come perform for your union, school, event, etc.
- Visit the Poster Nation web page and join the postering campaign.
- Host a workshop.
- Spread the word; get others to use the cookbook or order their own copies.
- Come visit us or contact us at:

37 Temple Place, 5th Floor
Boston, MA 02111
617/423-2148 • 617/423-0191 (fax)
stw@stw.org • www.stw.org

I am interested in the following:

- ❐ Becoming a member. ($25/year; includes newsletter)
- ❐ Getting trained to give educational workshops.
- ❐ Getting involved in Art for a Fair Economy in my area.
- ❐ Hosting a program: educational workshop • performance • creative action workshop (Please circle one or more.)
- ❐ Getting involved with PosterNation.
- ❐ Receiving a list of resources.

Name: ______________________________

Organization: ______________________________

Address: ______________________________

Phone: home: ____________________ work: ____________________

Fax: ____________________ email: ____________________

Mail & pay: United for a Fair Economy, 37 Temple Place, 5th Floor, Boston, MA 02111
617/423-2148 • 617/423-0191 (fax) • stw@stw.org • www.stw.org

I am interested in the following:

- ❐ Ordering more copies of *The Activist Cookbook.*

How many? ________ x ($16 for 1-5)* ($13 for 5-15) ($10 for 15+) = $________

Name: ______________________________

Organization: ______________________________

Address: ______________________________

Phone: home: ____________________ work: ____________________

Fax: ____________________ email: ____________________

Mail & pay: United for a Fair Economy, 37 Temple Place, 5th Floor, Boston, MA 02111
617/423-2148 • 617/423-0191 (fax) • stw@stw.org • www.stw.org

* all prices already include shipping & handling